GW01032990

For Chloé

Methuen/Moonlight
First published 1983 by Editions Gallimard
First published 1984 in Great Britain by Methuen
Children's Books Ltd, 11 New Fetter Lane, London EC4
in association with Moonlight Publishing Ltd
131 Kensington Church Street, London W8

Printed in Italy by La Editoriale Libraria

ISBN 0 907144 57 8

SUMMER

DISCOVERERS

by Laurence Ottenheimer
adapted and edited by Alex Campbell
illustrations by Jean Claverie

methuen moonlight

O the sky's an umbrella of sea-blue air
With a handle brightly pearled;
It opens up on everywhere,
It opens on the world.

William Jay Smith

This book belongs to ....

Haytime

Flowery banks,
A-drone with bees,
Dreaming cattle
Under trees:

Song-birds pipe
A merry tune —
This is summer,
This is June

Irene F. Pawsey

It's Midsummer Day
And they're cutting the hay
Down in the meadow over the
way,
The children all run
For a frolic, and fun —
For haytime is playtime out in
the sun.

It's Midsummer Day
And they're making the hay
Down in the meadow all
golden and gay,
They're tossing it high
Beneath the June sky,
And the hay rakes are spreading
it out to dry.

Irene F. Pawsey

June

Summer begins at the summer solstice. This is the longest day — and shortest night — of the year. It generally occurs on 21 June.

Summer ends at the autumn equinox. This usually occurs on 22 September and is one of the two occasions in the year when day and night are of equal length. Between the summer solstice and the autumn equinox the nights grow longer and days shorter.

21 As the days begin to shorten,
The heat begins to scorch them.

22

23

24 Mid-summer and St John's Day

Mid-summer's Eve was once a magic time: people believed that on this night ghosts, goblins and fairies became visible to ordinary mortals.

Mid-summer used to be celebrated with huge bonfires and torchlit processions in honour of the sun. Later it also became the festival of St John the Baptist. One old custom was that young men and girls leaped over the embers of a fire holding hands.

The grass is happy
When the June sun roasts the
foxgloves in the hedges.
Ted Hughes

Calm weather in
June
Sets corn in tune.

25

26

27 *I saw the sea put on its dress*
Of blue mid-summer loveliness,

28 *And heard the trees begin to stir*
Green arms of pine and juniper.

29 *I heard the wind call out and say:*
"Get up, my dear, it is today!"

30

Rachel Field

July

Early in July sunrise is at about 4.45a.m. and sunset at about 9.20p.m. Every day sunrise is a little later, sunset a little earlier, by less than a minute each.

1
2

If the first of July it be rainy weather,
It will rain more or less for four weeks together.

3
4
5

We'll talk of sunshine and of song,
And summer days, when we are young.

William Wordsworth

6

7

Whatever July and August do not boil, September cannot fry.

8
9
10
11

No, they never see July,
no matter how they try

No they never ever,
never ever never see July.

Shel Silverstein

Who are they? (uəɯʍouS)

Then came hot July,
boyling like to fire.

Edmund Spenser

12

13

14

High summer on the mountains
And on the clover leas,
And on the local sidings,
And on the rhubarb leaves.

Brass bands in all the valleys
Blaring defiant tunes,
Crowds, acclaiming carnival,
Prize pigs and wooden spoons.

Dust on shabby hedgerows
Behind the colliery wall,
Dust on rail and girder
And tram and prop and all.

High summer on the slag heaps
And on polluted streams,
And old men in the
morning
Telling the town their
dreams.

Idris Davies

Hot July brings cooling showers,
Apricots, and gillyflowers.

Sara Coleridge

15 St Swithin's Day, if ye do rain,
For 40 days it will remain.

16

17

18 *A fishing pole's a curious thing;*
It's made of just a stick and string;

19 *A boy at one end and a wish,*
And on the other end a fish.

20 Mary Carolyn Davies

21 Look out for the lovely flowers
of the water lily in July.

22

23 *When the thunder stalks the sky,*
When tickle-footed walks the fly,

24 *When shirt is wet and throat is dry,*
Look, my darling, that's July.

25 Ogden Nash

Girls scream,
Boys shout,
Dogs bark,
School's out.

W. H. Davies

26 In July shear your rye.

27

28

29

30

31

Apples in the orchard
Mellowing one by one;
Strawberries upturning
Soft cheeks to the sun;
Roses faint with sweetness,
Lilies fair of face,
Drowsy scents and murmurs
Haunting every place;
Lengths of golden sunshine,
Moonlight bright as day —
Don't you think that summer's
Pleasanter than May?

Thomas Bailey Aldrich

August

Early in August sunrise is at about 5.20a.m. and sunset at about 8.50p.m. Each day the sunrise is about a minute later, sunset a minute earlier.

1	Lammas Day
2	
3	After Lammas corn ripens as much by night as by day.
4	
5 6	*All things that love the sun are out of doors;* *The sky rejoices in the morning's birth.* William Wordsworth
7	
8	August ripens, September gathers in.
9	
10	Dry August and warm Doth harvest no harm.
11	

August brings the sheaves of corn.
Then the harvest home is borne.

Sara Coleridge

12

13

14

15 On St Mary's Day sunshine
Brings much and good wine.

When the butterfly comes, comes also the summer.
(Zuñi Indians)

In the morning, very early,
That's the time I love to go
Barefoot where the fern grows
curly
And grass is cool between
each toe,
On a summer morning-O!
On a summer morning!

Rachel Field

16

17

18

Sing a song of picnics,
Bread and butter spread,
Greenery all round about,
And cherries overhead.

Rachel Field

19	
20 21	To keep your drinks cool on a picnic, put them in a pond or stream. But make sure they are not swept away!
22	
23	
24 25	All the tears that St. Swithin can cry St. Bartlemy's dusty mantle wipes dry.
26 27	Take a notebook and pencil with you. Make notes and drawings of what you see: insects, flowers, birds. . .
28	
29 30	*So it falls that all men are* *With fine weather happier far.* King Alfred
31	

September

September blow soft till the fruit's in the loft.

Early in September sunrise is at about 6.10a.m. and sunset at about 7.50p.m. Until the autumn equinox the days grow shorter by about a minute in the morning and a minute in the evening.

1 Fair on the first of September, fair for the month.

2

3

4 September is autumn's May
French proverb

5

6

7

8

9

10

11

Here comes summer,
Here comes summer,

Chirping robin, budding rose,
Here comes summer,

Here comes summer,
Gentle showers, summer clothes.

Here comes summer,
Here comes summer —

Whoosh — shiver — there it goes
Shel Silverstein

Warm September brings the fruit;
Sportsmen then begin to shoot.
Sara Coleridge

12

13

14

15 *This day is said to be fine in six years out of seven* T. Forster

16

17

Nine-o'clock Bell!
Nine-o'clock Bell!
All the small children
and big ones as
well
Eleanor Farjeon

In the last week of the holidays
I was feeling glum.
I could hardly wait for school to
start;
Neither could mum.
Allan Ahlberg

18

19

20 The 20th, 21st, 22nd September rule the weather for October, November, December

21 First day of Autumn

Stars in the summer sky

Looking north

1. Great Bear 2. Little Bear 3. Cassiopeia 4. Andromeda
5. Capella 6. Lyra 7. Vega 8. N. Crown 9. Scales
10. Scorpio 11. Sagittarius 12. Capricorn 13. Delphinus

Looking south

The Milky Way

On a clear night you can often see a faint band of light crossing the sky. This is the Milky Way. It is made up of stars, perhaps as many as 200,000 million, connected to each other by forces of gravity. Its stars are so many billions of miles away that they appear tiny.

The night will never stay

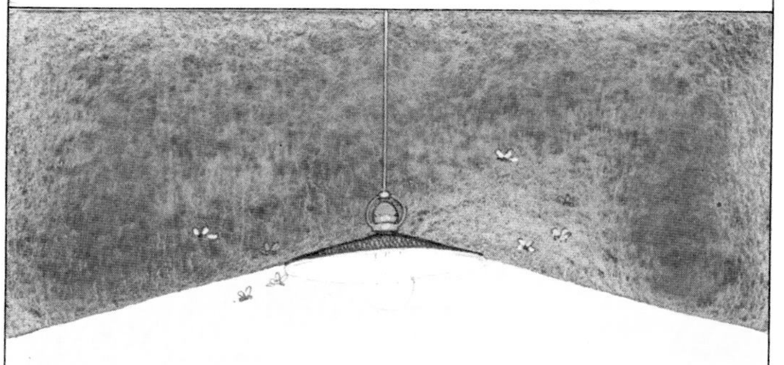

The night will never stay,
The night will still go by,
Though with a million stars
You pin it to the sky;
Though you bind it with
the blowing wind
And buckle it with the moon,
The night will slip away
Like sorrow or a tune.

Eleanor Farjeon

Shooting stars

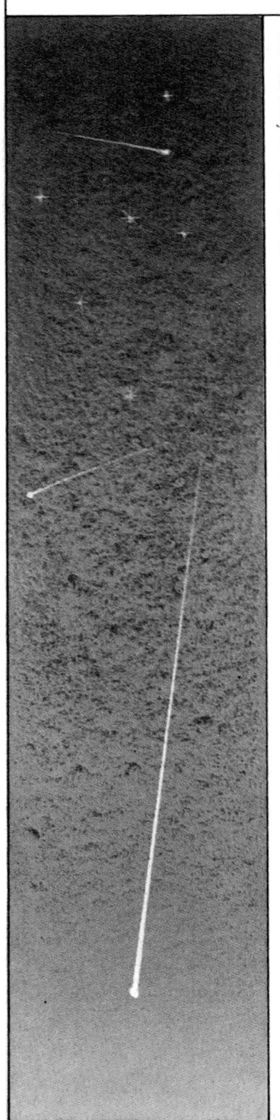

Summer is a good time to look out for shooting stars. The Earth, on its journey round the sun, is moving then through a zone where they are plentiful. But what we call shooting stars are not really stars at all. They are **meteors.**

Meteors are bits of dust or rock from outer space. They become burning hot when they enter and fall through the atmosphere that surrounds the Earth. If you are lucky, you might see one of the rare, brilliant fireballs, caused by larger meteors, composed of rock or iron.

Most meteors burn themselves up in the atmosphere but sometimes a fireball reaches the Earth, most often falling into the sea. A fallen meteor is called a meteorite.

Rarely, **comets** are seen moving across the night sky. Comets are thought to consist of dust, ice and gas. Most comets have been seen only once in recorded history, but a few, such as Halley's comet, visible in 1986, have shorter orbits around the sun and reappear regularly over the Earth.

Under cloak of night

Quietly down the sky,
quietly skirting the meadow,
the Lady of Night slips by,
trailing her purple shadow,
moving without a sound
of footsteps or garments sweeping,
wrapping her cloak around
birds in the treetops, sleeping.
Aileen Fisher

The sun

The sun is our closest star. It is an enormous ball of burning gases which gives us light and heat. Without it the earth would be a cold dark planet on which nothing lived or grew.

The sun is about 93 million miles from the earth. Its light takes about 8 minutes to reach us. Even though the sun is so far away, its rays are so powerful that, on a hot day, they can burn your skin if you sunbathe for too long, and can even blind you if you stare directly into the sun.

Scientists believe that the sun is about 4,600,000,000 years old and that it will shine for at least as many years again.

I think life would be more fun
Without the simmering summer sun.
Ogden Nash

From earliest time, people realized the sun's importance to the Earth. But they did not know all that we know about it and many worshipped it as a god. They found various ways of explaining its daily journey across the sky. The Greek sun god, Helios, drove his chariot across the sky. The Egyptian sun god, Re, sailed his boat: he was young when he set out at dawn, grown up by noon, and old at sunset when he arrived in the west.

In America, the Plains Indians used to hold a sun dance lasting several days. The men painted their bodies and danced facing the sun, to the music of whistles made of eagle bone.

The sun, they say, is very big,
a star that shines by day,
much bigger than the whole big earth,
oh, very much, they say.

But when I'm hiding in a field
of clover-smelling hay,
a single little clover plant
can hide the sun away.
Aileen Fisher

Why is it hot in summer?

We have seasons because the Earth is tilted.

Imagine a line running through the centre of the Earth from the North to the South Pole. We call this imaginary line the Earth's axis. The Earth is tilted on its axis, which means that half of the Earth is nearer to the sun around which it travels. It takes the Earth a year to complete one orbit around the sun. When the northern hemisphere is tilted towards the sun, it receives more of the sun's heat and we have summer. Meanwhile it is winter in the southern hemisphere, which is tilted away from the sun.

Six months later, when the Earth has moved halfway round the sun, the northern hemisphere is tilted away from the sun and the southern hemisphere towards it.

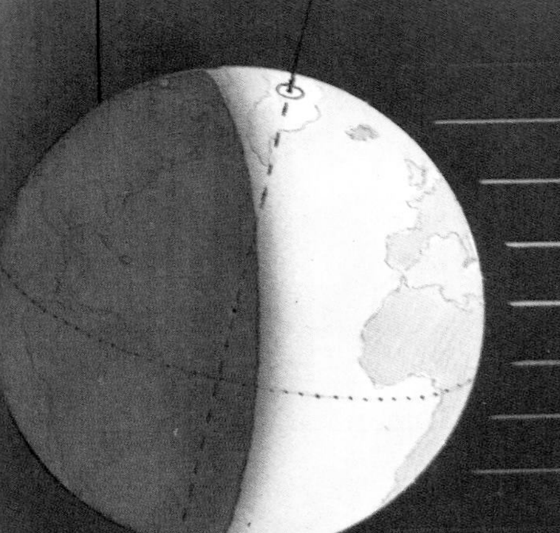

Shadows

On a sunny day, shadows are formed by anything that blocks the sun's rays.

When you stand in the sun, your body stops some of the sun's rays from reaching the ground. Your shadow shows the area the sun cannot reach because of you.

Shadows shrink and grow during the day according to the sun's position in the sky. Around midday the sun is overhead: its rays shine down directly onto your head and shoulders which cast almost no shadow, or a small one, like a dwarf's. In the early morning and evening the sun shines low in the sky: its rays slant towards you, striking the full length of your body which casts a long shadow, like a giant's.

Never in his life has
the sun seen shade,
Never in his life seen a
shadow where it falls.

A. E. Housman

A shadow always lies in the direction opposite to the sun.

I have a little shadow that goes in and out with
me,
And what can be the use of him is more than I can
see.
He is very, very like me from the heels up to the
head;
And I see him jump before me, when I jump into
my bed.

The funniest thing about him is the way he likes
to grow —
Not at all like proper children, which is
always very slow;
For he sometimes shoots up
taller like an india-rubber
ball,
And he sometimes gets so little
that there's none of him
at all.

Robert Louis Stevenson

How to make a sundial

You can make a sundial out of a flowerpot with a hole in its base. Turn the pot upside down and fix a stick upright through the hole. Then set the pot in a place that gets the sun throughout the day. The stick will cast a shadow which will gradually move round the base of the pot, like the hand of a clock, according to the position of the sun in the sky.

Checking the time by an accurate clock, every hour mark the place where the shadow lies on the base of the pot and write the time beside it. Provided that you do not move your sundial, it will tell you the time on a sunny day.

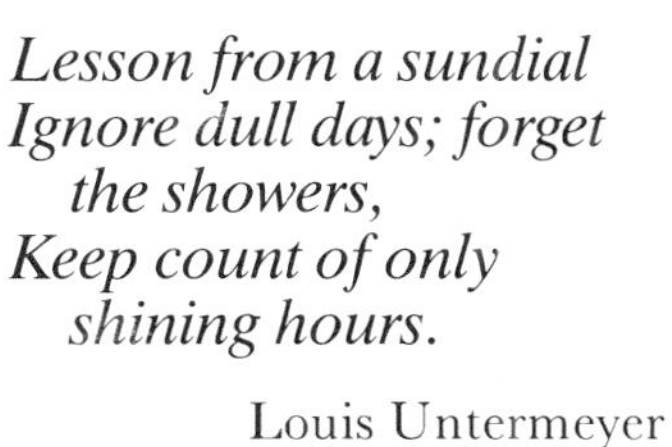

Lesson from a sundial
Ignore dull days; forget
the showers,
Keep count of only
shining hours.

Louis Untermeyer

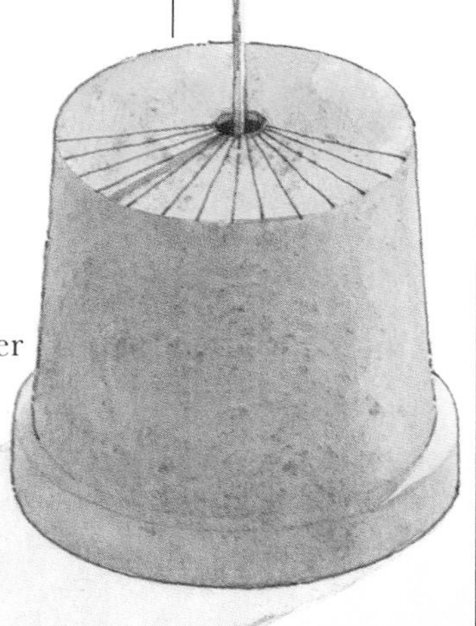

Thunderstorms

The thunder is
rumbling
And crashing and
crumbling —
Will silence return
nevermore.
James Russell Lowell

Thunderstorms happen most frequently after a sunny summer morning when the air around us has grown hot and humid. This hot air then rises to meet layers of cold air which cool it suddenly. The moisture in the air condenses: tiny drops of water form and make clouds.

At the same time as the hot air rushes upwards, cold air moves into its place and currents of hot and cold air circulate and jostle with each other in the atmosphere.

These currents agitate the clouds, so that the drops of water in them are rubbed against each other. This friction makes electricity. Lightning is a huge spark of electricity which suddenly shoots out of a cloud.

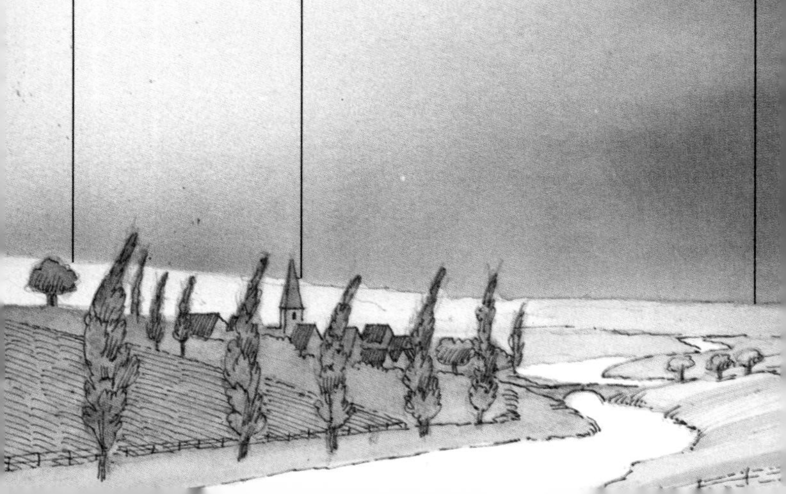

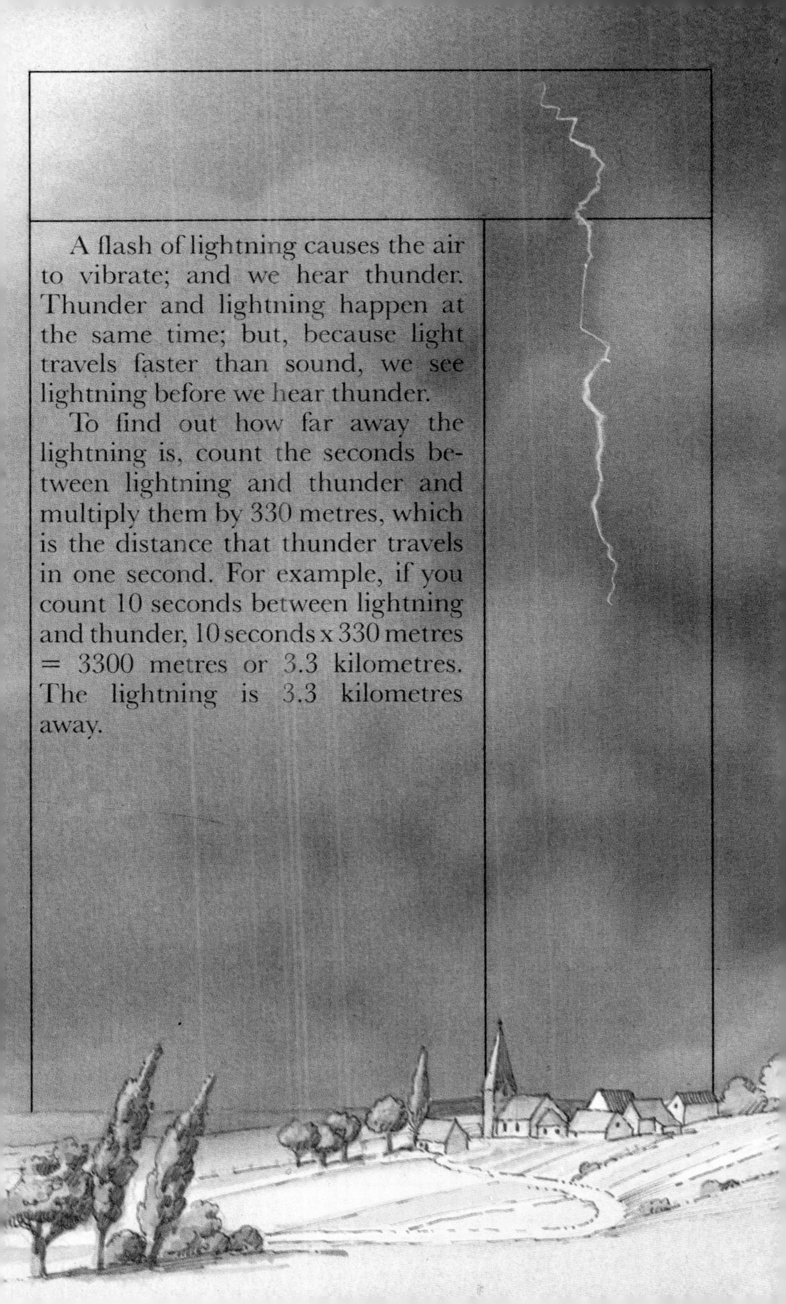

A flash of lightning causes the air to vibrate; and we hear thunder. Thunder and lightning happen at the same time; but, because light travels faster than sound, we see lightning before we hear thunder.

To find out how far away the lightning is, count the seconds between lightning and thunder and multiply them by 330 metres, which is the distance that thunder travels in one second. For example, if you count 10 seconds between lightning and thunder, 10 seconds x 330 metres = 3300 metres or 3.3 kilometres. The lightning is 3.3 kilometres away.

Nature's weather forecasters

If bees stay at home
Rain will soon come;
If they fly away,
Fine will be the day.
Anon

Expect rain when:
— bees stay in the hive;
— hens scratch themselves, roll in the dust, call their chicks or take shelter;
— donkeys shake their ears and bray without stopping;
— cows lick themselves;
— horses drum their hooves and stretch out their necks, breathing noisily;
— butterflies fly near windows;

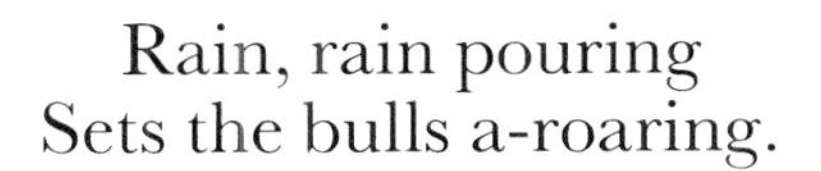
Rain, rain pouring
Sets the bulls a-roaring.

— worms and snails are out in plenty;
— frogs and toads croak by day;
— fish leap and bite more than usual;
— swallows fly low;
— crows fly in groups;
— moles dig hard and raise mole-hills.

Plants and the sun

To live and grow, most plants need both sun and water; but too much sun can cause plants to wither and die. Some plants have ways of protecting themselves against the sun's heat.

Plants like **gorse** (2), **broom** (3) and **heather** (4) have small leaves, which absorb less sunlight than the larger leaves of some plants. Others, such as **laurel** (6) and **olive** (7), have leaves with a waxy surface which protects them from drying out in the sun.

Cactuses have swollen stems which act like reservoirs, supplying

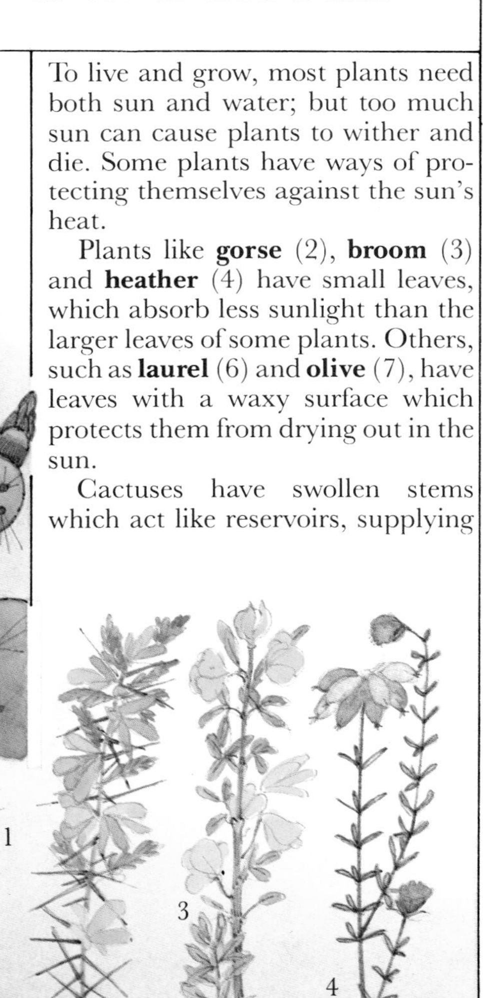

the plant with water through months, even years, of drought. The **prickly pear** (1) is an example.

Many species curl up their leaves, which stay moist on the inside; *couch grass* does this, for example, as does *smooth-stalked meadow grass,* whose flowers open only at night.

Most plants, however, grow towards the light of the sun. Many, such as the **sunflower** (5), even turn their heads to follow the sun's movement during the day.

The trees in their green

1 Walnut
2 Hazel
3 Poplar
4 Plane

9

3

2

8

1

3

4

5

2

Summer has spread a cool, green tent
Upon the bare poles of
this tree;
Where 'tis a joy to sit
all day,
And hear the
small birds' melody.

W. H. Davies

Summer visitors

Summer days for me
When every leaf is on its
tree . . .

And blue-black beetles
transact business,
And gnats fly in a host,
And furry caterpillars
hasten
That no time be lost,
And moths grow fat and
thrive,
And ladybirds arrive.

Christina Rossetti

Insect-spotting

Here are some of the insects you can see in summer. They lay eggs and hatch in enormous numbers when the weather is warm. One queen bee alone can lay 1500 eggs a day.

Wasps (1) build a nest each year. There they rear the larvae that hatch from the queen wasp's eggs and grow into adult wasps. The larvae are fed on nectar from flowers and on other insects, which the female wasp can paralyse with the poisonous sting that lies at the base of her abdomen.

Honey bees (2) are social insects, as are all the insects on this page: they live in colonies. Each colony has one bee that lays eggs: the queen; a relatively small number of males, called drones; and many thousands of female workers that cannot lay eggs: they clean and defend the hive, build the honeycomb, care for the larvae and gather pollen and nectar from flowers, which they feed to the larvae or make into honey.

Bumble bees (3) have hairy bodies and feed from flowers.

A hornet (4) is a large wasp with a very painful sting.

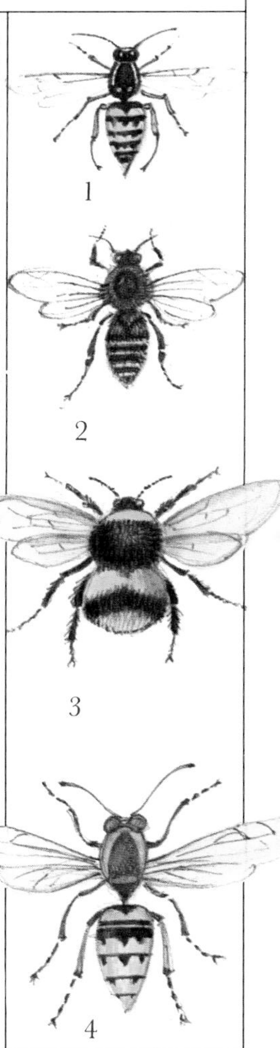

Calico Drum,
The Grasshoppers come,
The Butterfly, Beetle, and Bee . . .
Edward Lear

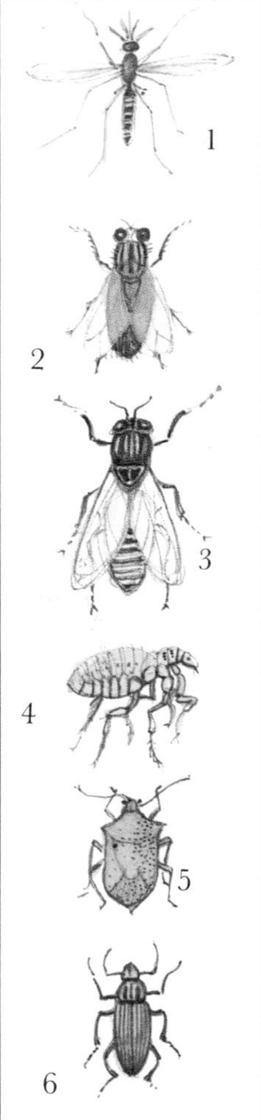

The mosquito (1) likes to live near water. It flies mostly in the evening, early morning or when the sky is overcast. Only the female "bites": the blood she sucks nourishes her developing eggs.

The housefly (2) has pads of tiny hairs on its feet: with these it can cling to anything, walking on ceilings or up walls. The female lays about 200 eggs which hatch into maggots.

The horsefly (3) is often found near grazing animals. The female sucks blood from animals or people, leaving a big swelling on the skin.

The flea (4) is found on dogs, cats, pigs and humans, too. It jumps and is hard to catch.

This green shield bug (5) is often found in large numbers on hazel trees.

The pine weevil (6) lives in coniferous woods. It does much damage by feeding on young pine shoots.

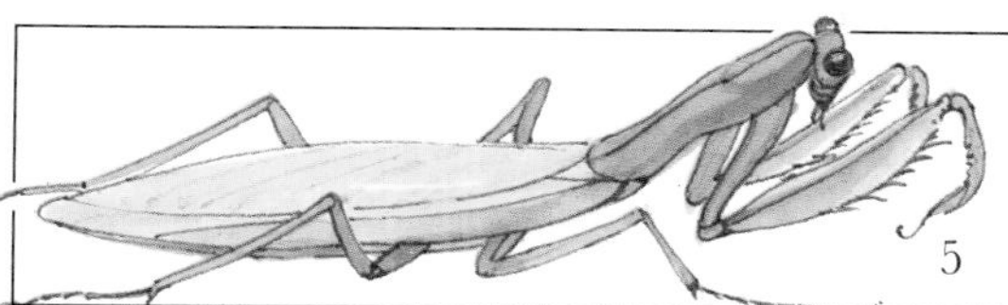

This **ground beetle** (1) hides underground by day. At night it comes out into the fields to chase other insects, worms and snails.

The earwig (2) is a harmless insect which spends the day in cracks and corners of the house. The old belief that it likes to crawl into people's ears is completely untrue.

The rose-chafer beetle (3) is found on flowers and flowering shrubs. It feeds mainly on petals.

The stag-beetle (4) lives on old oaks. It is the largest of the European insects but is becoming rare.

The praying mantis (5) is found in the warmer countries of the world. It catches other insects with its front legs and devours them with its powerful jaws.

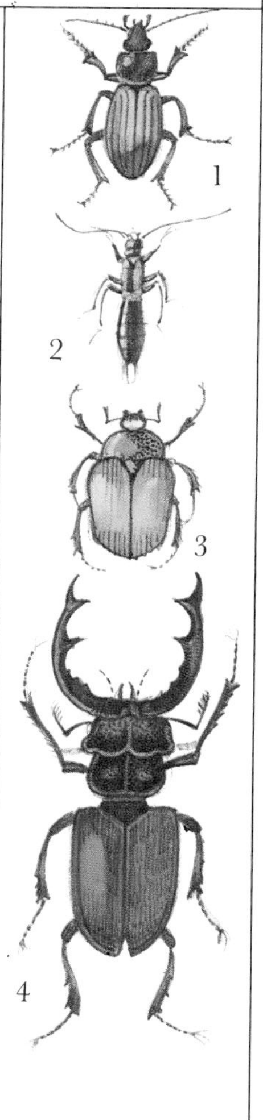

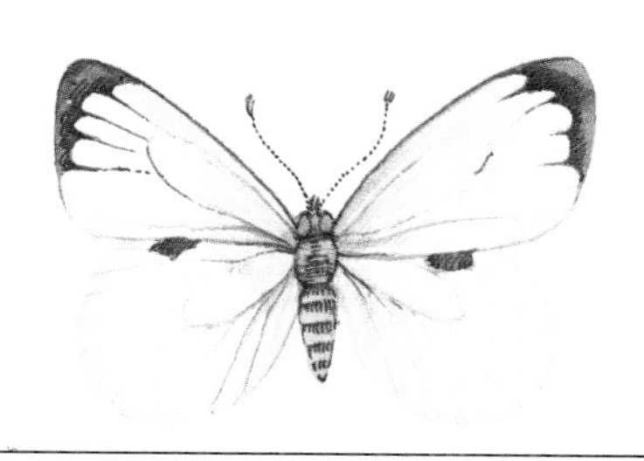

Ant colonies

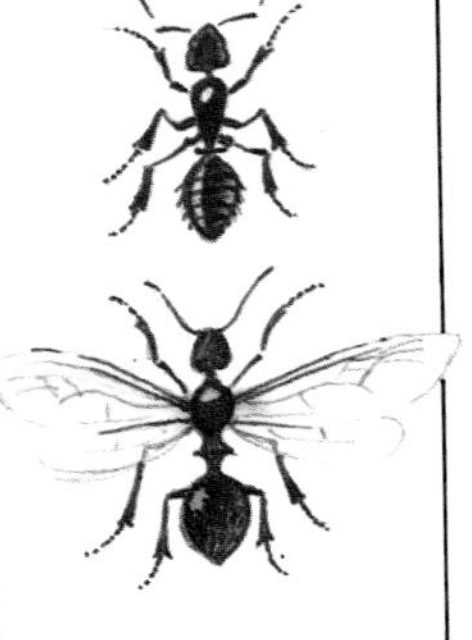

An ants' nest is a miniature city. Inside there may be 30 or 40 storeys of underground chambers, linked by tiny passageways along which the ants come and go. The heap of twigs, dead leaves and pine needles at the entrance stops the rain from getting in.

Long lines of worker ants leave the nest in search of food. When an ant finds prey, such as a large beetle, that is too big for one ant to manage, it signals to another ant with its antennae: together they drag the beetle home. Sometimes an ant returns to the nest to fetch reinforcements, leaving a scented trail so that it can find the way back.

Other workers keep busy underground: some build and clean the nest; some stand by the entrance to guard it; some look after the eggs and larvae. In the morning they carry the eggs to the warmer upper chambers; in the evening they carry them down to avoid the damp. The queen ant, meanwhile, is busy laying more eggs.

The ants are walking under the ground,
And the pigeons are flying over the steeple,
And in between are the people.

Elizabeth Madox Roberts

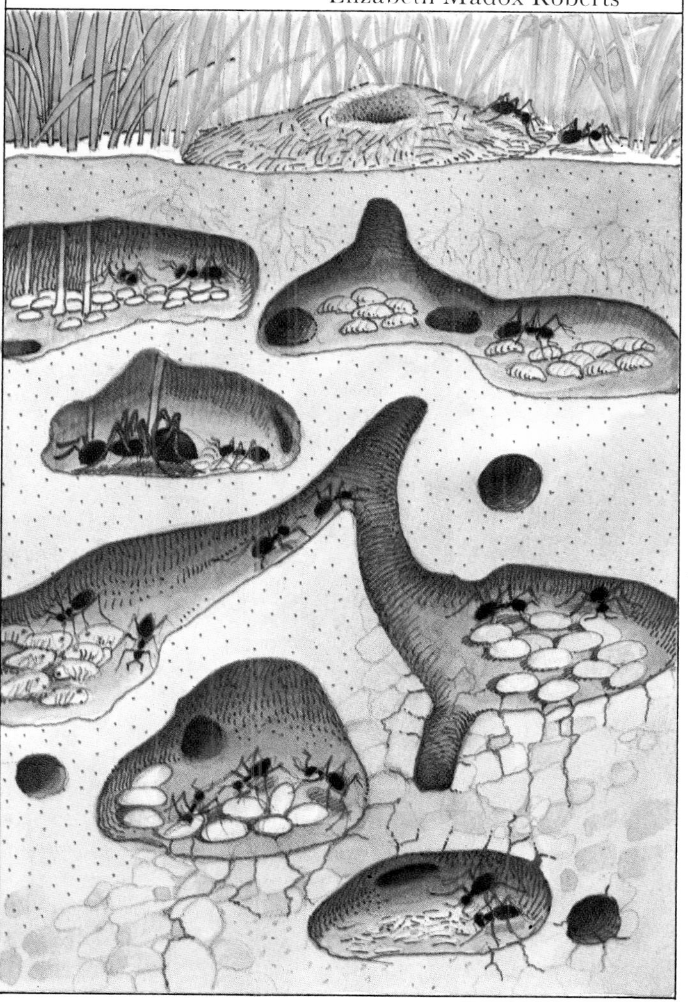

Glow-worms and fireflies

On a summer's evening, just after night has fallen, look out for tiny lights in the grass. These are from female glow-worms. They cannot fly, and so they climb a low plant to display the yellow-green light on the underside of their abdomen. This helps the males, who are flying above, to find them in the dark.

Adult glow-worms do not eat. They live only eight or nine days. But their larvae have huge appetites: they inject slugs and snails with a poisonous liquid which sends them to sleep and makes their flesh liquid and easy to swallow.

. . . Many a glow-worm in the shade
Lights up her love-torch.

S. T. Coleridge

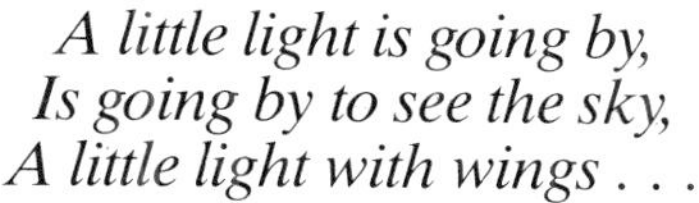

A little light is going by,
Is going by to see the sky,
A little light with wings . . .

Fireflies and glow-worms are really beetles that make light. There are many kinds, mostly found in hot countries. Once, in China and Japan, poor students used to read at night by the light of fireflies; and in Brazil people lit their homes with firefly lanterns. Sometimes frogs shine at night because they have eaten so many fireflies.

. . . I never could have thought of
it,
To have a little bug all lit
And made to go on wings.

Elizabeth Madox Roberts

Insect musicians

Some insects make light to attract their mates. Others make music.

On a sunny summer day you may hear the chirp of the male **grasshopper** (2), who makes the noise by rubbing his hind legs against tiny serrations on his wings. The females approach when they hear the chirp of their own species of grasshopper. Each species makes a different sound.

Crickets (3) chirp by rubbing parts of their wings together.

Cicadas (1) are commonly found in hot countries, but one species is known in southern England. The male vibrates a membrane on either side of his body to make a loud noise like a drum.

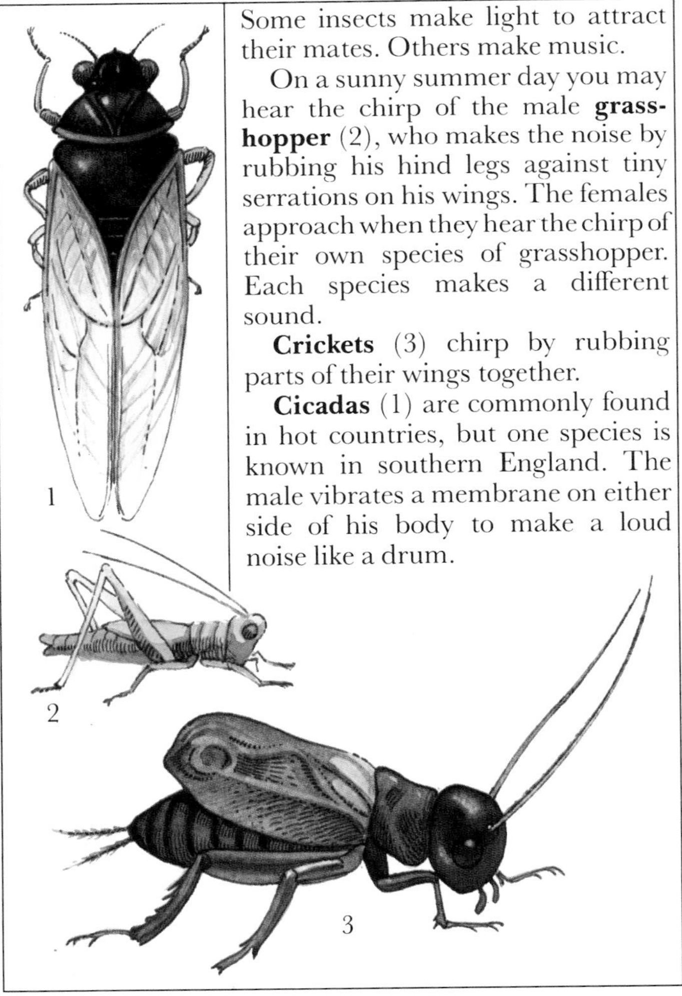

The lizard

The lizard loves to bask in the sun: it keeps very still, poised to catch a spider, grasshopper or other insect on its sticky tongue.

As soon as a lizard is disturbed, it darts into hiding. Do not try to catch one by the tail: it will leave its tail in your hand and soon grow another.

Most lizards lay eggs. But some, like the common lizard, give birth to live young in the summer, in litters of five to ten. In winter lizards hibernate.

The lizard is a funny
thing.
He has a snaky head,
A snaky tail beside —
and yet
He is a quad-ru-ped.
Abbie Farwell Brown

Dragonflies

The dragonflies,
All flying in the same
direction,
In the rays of the
setting sun.

Rungai

Dragonflies, with their brightly coloured wings, are most often found by ponds and rivers. They are among the fastest of insects: some can fly at over 50 miles an hour.

The dragonfly has a huge appetite. In half an hour it can eat its own weight in other insects, especially mosquitoes, which are its favourite food.

The dragonfly was sometimes called the 'devil's darning needle' because of the superstition that it could sew up the eyes, mouth and ears of a sleeping child.

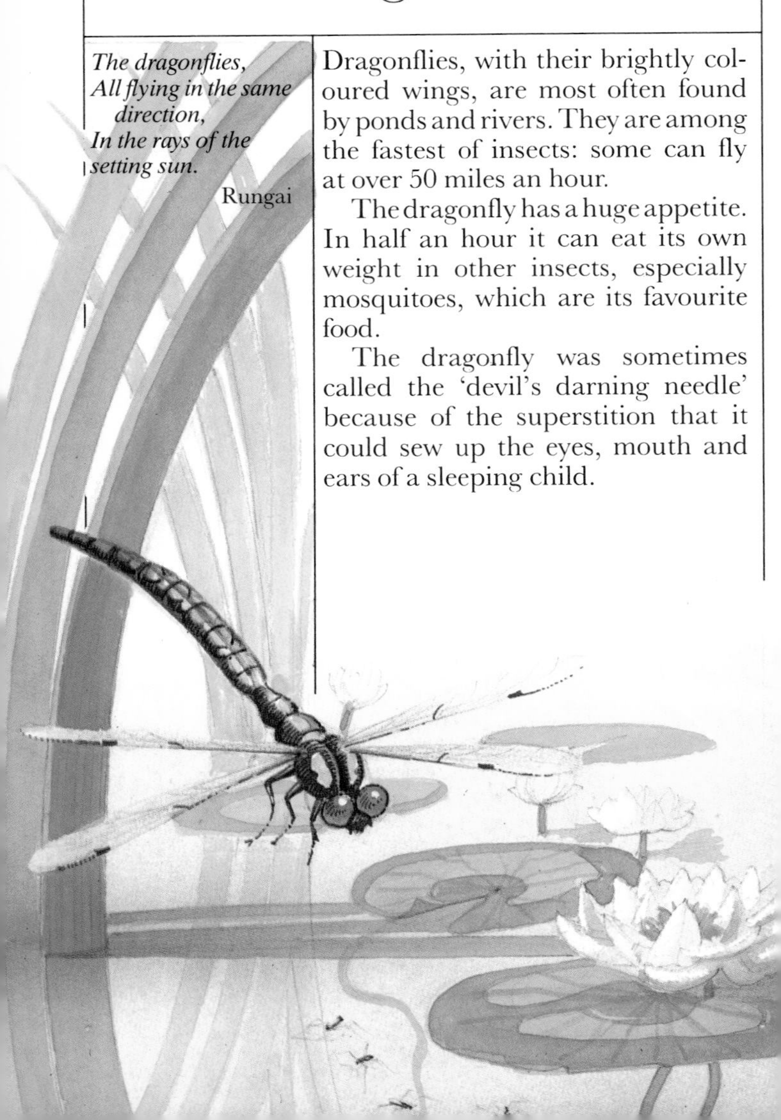

Freshwater fish

In summer there is plenty for fish to eat in ponds and rivers. Some feed on water weeds, others on worms, insects and other fish. The pike will even eat frogs, voles and ducklings. Many fish build up stores of fat which help to keep them alive through the winter, when food is scarce.

You can tell a fish's age by counting the dark and light areas on one of its scales. The dark area shows winter growth, which is slow. The wider, light area shows summer growth, which is faster.

Most fish spawn in the warm months of the year, leaving huge numbers of eggs in the water. But many of the young fish fall prey to other creatures before they are full grown. They are eaten by birds, other fish and even water beetles.

In this quiet pool
fish
glide
bugs
ride
snakes
slide
turtles
hide

Lilian Moore

My eyes are buried in the cold pond, under
The cold spread leaves; my thoughts
are silver-wet.

E. J. Scovell

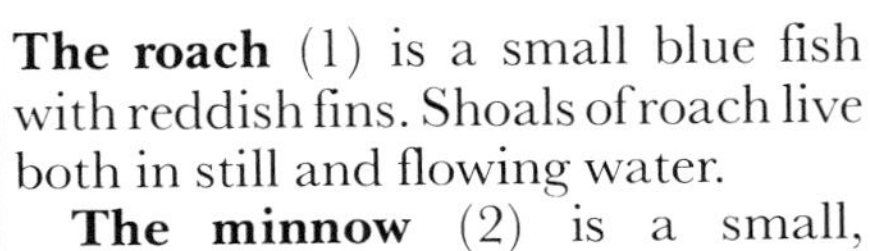

The roach (1) is a small blue fish with reddish fins. Shoals of roach live both in still and flowing water.

The minnow (2) is a small, slender fish found in the shallow parts of ponds and rivers, often in schools.

The gudgeon (3) is a little fish that lives in clear rivers with gravel beds. It feeds on worms, insect larvae and shellfish on the river bed.

The trout (4) also likes clean water. The dark spots on its skin act as camouflage. It often jumps out of the water to catch insects.

The tench (5) is a medium-sized fish with a dark green back and distinctively rounded tail. It likes

Swarms of minnows show their little heads,
Staying their wavy bodies 'gainst the streams,
To taste the luxury of sunny beams
Tempered with coolness.
John Keats

slow, weedy, muddy water. It stirs up the mud when hunting for food, and this causes bubbles of air to rise to the surface.

The bleak (6) is a little fish that makes lots of small circular ripples on the water as it feeds on insects near the surface.

The carp (7) likes quiet, muddy, weedy water. It can live up to 40 years and grows enormous, feeding on plants, worms and insects in the mud. The carp swims slowly: you can work out its route by following the movement of the water weeds.

The perch (8) is a medium-sized fish with black stripes on its back. It likes to live in still water among plants and is extremely greedy.

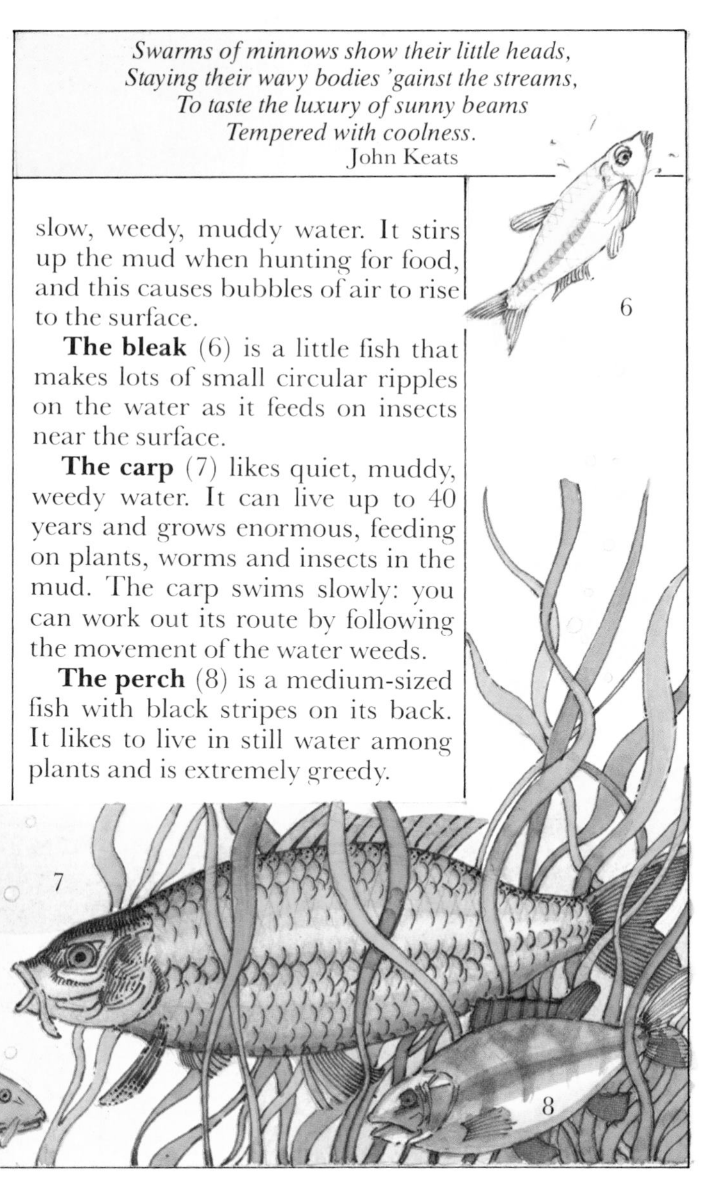

The adder

Can you tell the difference between the poisonous adder and the harmless grass snake? Both of them like warmth and often bask in the sun. But only the adder is dangerous.

Here are some differences to watch for:

The adder has a zig-zag pattern down its back, a triangular-shaped head, a raised snout, oval pupils to its eyes and a thick, heavy tail. It is less than 80cm long.

Adders like dry heath and grassland. They feed on young birds, lizards, frogs, newts, mice and rats. The adder bites its prey with its poisonous fangs, then follows it till it dies.

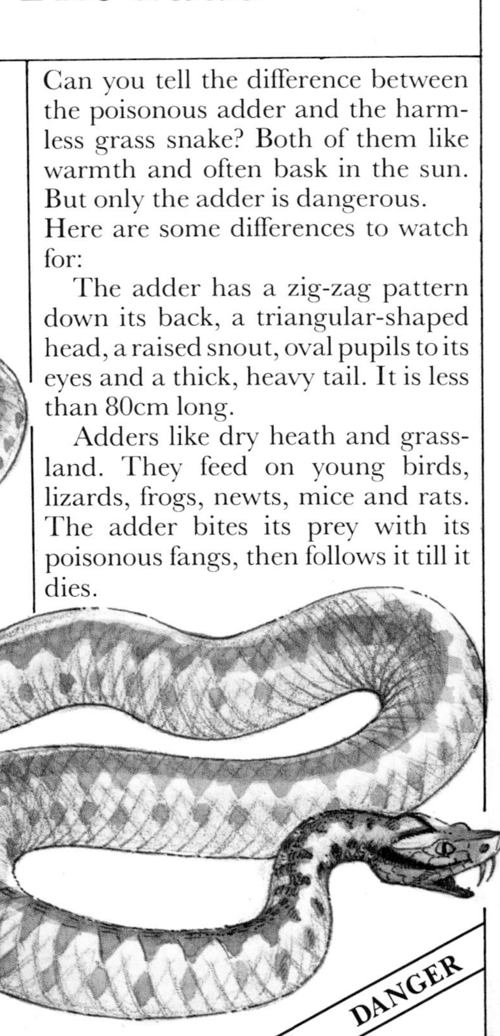

DANGER

The grass snake

The grass snake has no zig-zag pattern on its back. It has an oval head, round pupils to its eyes and a slender tail. It is more than 80cm long and hisses if attacked, having no real way of defending itself. It is a good swimmer and likes to live near water, feeding on frogs, fish, newts, small birds and eggs.

Birds' feet

The feet of each species of bird are particularly suited to its way of life.

The coal tit (1), like many birds that perch, has short legs with four clawed toes: the back toe curls round to meet the three front toes, allowing the bird to grip the branch.

The woodpecker (2) climbs trees, gripping the bark with its strong claws: two toes point forwards and two point back.

The meadow pippit (3) does not climb trees but lives on the ground in rough open country, such as downs or moorland. It has a long back toe that helps it balance when it walks or runs.

The duck (4), like many water birds, has webbed feet which act as paddles in the water.

The reed warbler (5) builds its nest in the reeds. Its long legs enable it to adopt various acrobatic positions on the reeds amongst which it lives.

The heron (6) does not swim. But with its long legs it can wade through water looking for fish, frogs and voles to eat.

Footprints in the sand

Birds leave footprints on the sand or on damp ground. Look at them carefully and see if you can identify them. Notice the position and shape of the toes, the width and length of the footprint, the marks of claws.

Perching birds

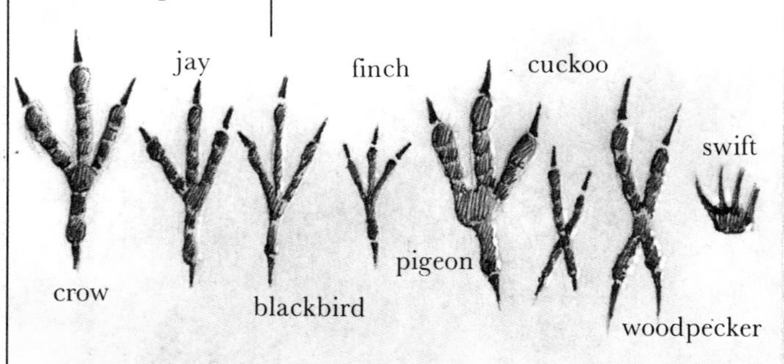

Ground birds

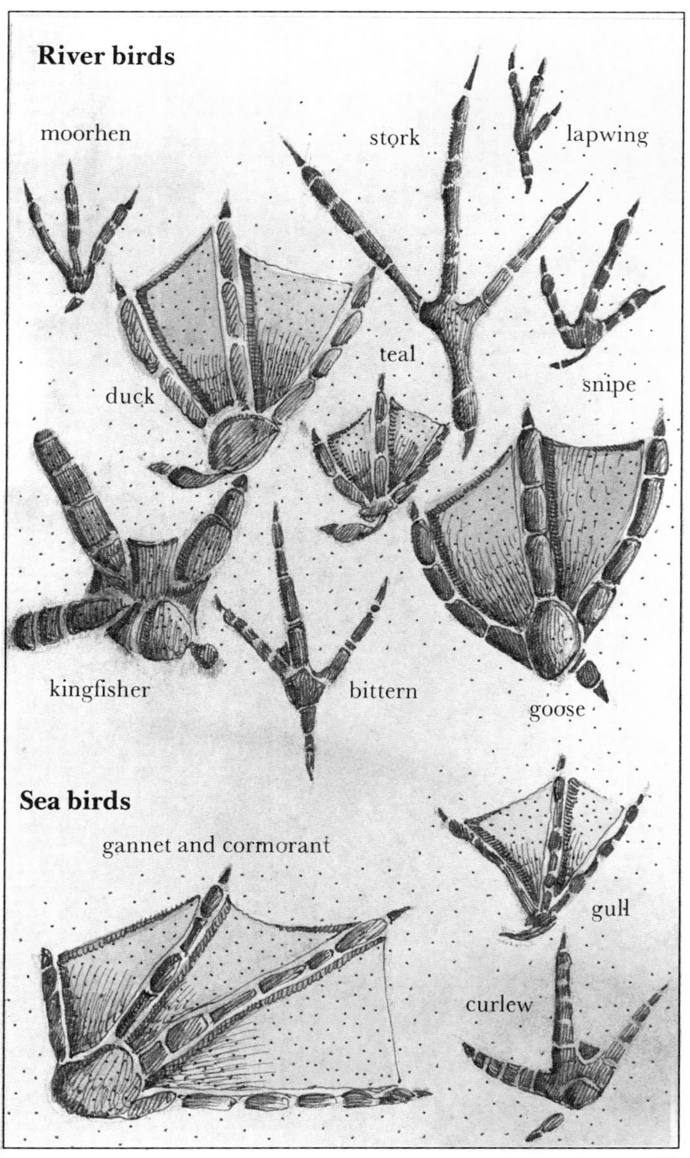
River birds
moorhen
stork
lapwing
teal
duck
snipe
kingfisher
bittern
goose
Sea birds
gannet and cormorant
gull
curlew

Beaks

Birds have plenty to eat in summer: insects, seeds, worms, fruit, fish, frogs, even small mammals. The shape of a bird's beak is often a clue to its feeding habits. While some, such as gulls and crows, will eat anything, others have special diets.

Seed and nut-eaters, such as finches and sparrows, have short, stout beaks to crack open their food. The hawfinch can even crack a cherry stone. The redpoll, another finch, likes the seeds of the birch and alder and some weeds.

Fruit-eaters have varied beaks. The thrush's is thinner and less powerful than a seed-eater's, but it serves several purposes: to catch insects and worms, to eat fruit and berries, and to knock snails against stones until they crack open.

The Vulture eats between his meals
And that's the reason why
He very, very rarely feels
As well as you and I.
Hilaire Belloc

Insect-eaters have thin beaks like pincers. Swallows and swifts feed entirely on insects. Robins eat insects, worms, fruit and seeds.

Fish-eaters, such as the kingfisher and heron, live on fish they have speared with their long, sharp dagger-like beaks. **Plant-eating** river birds have wide bills with which they can grip and crop water weeds or grass. The mallard feeds mainly on the buds, seeds and stems of plants in the water.

Meat-eaters, such as the eagle, owl and falcon, have hooked beaks with which to tear the flesh of mammals and other birds. The eagle will prey on hares and lambs, the owl on mice, rats and shrews.

Ducks' tails, drakes' tails,
Yellow feet a-quiver,
Yellow bills all out of sight
Busy in the river.
Kenneth Grahame

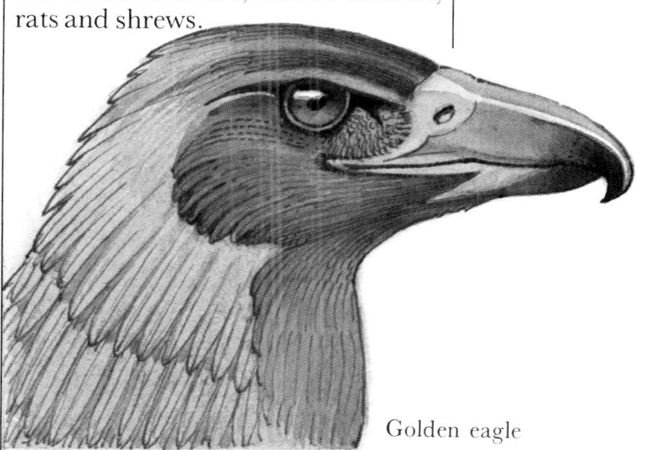

Golden eagle

Feathers

A large bird, such as a swan, may have as many as 25,000 feathers; a small song bird only 1500. Birds have fewer feathers in summer than in winter. Many species moult during summer, shedding their old feathers as new ones grow. Some species grow a set of new feathers in a month; others may take seven months.

The inner soft *down* feathers keep a bird warm. Over these lie small feathers called *coverts*, which overlap like tiles on a roof. Then, fastened to the wings and tail, are the long outer feathers called *pennae*. These are the bird's flight feathers.

For centuries, these long, stiff

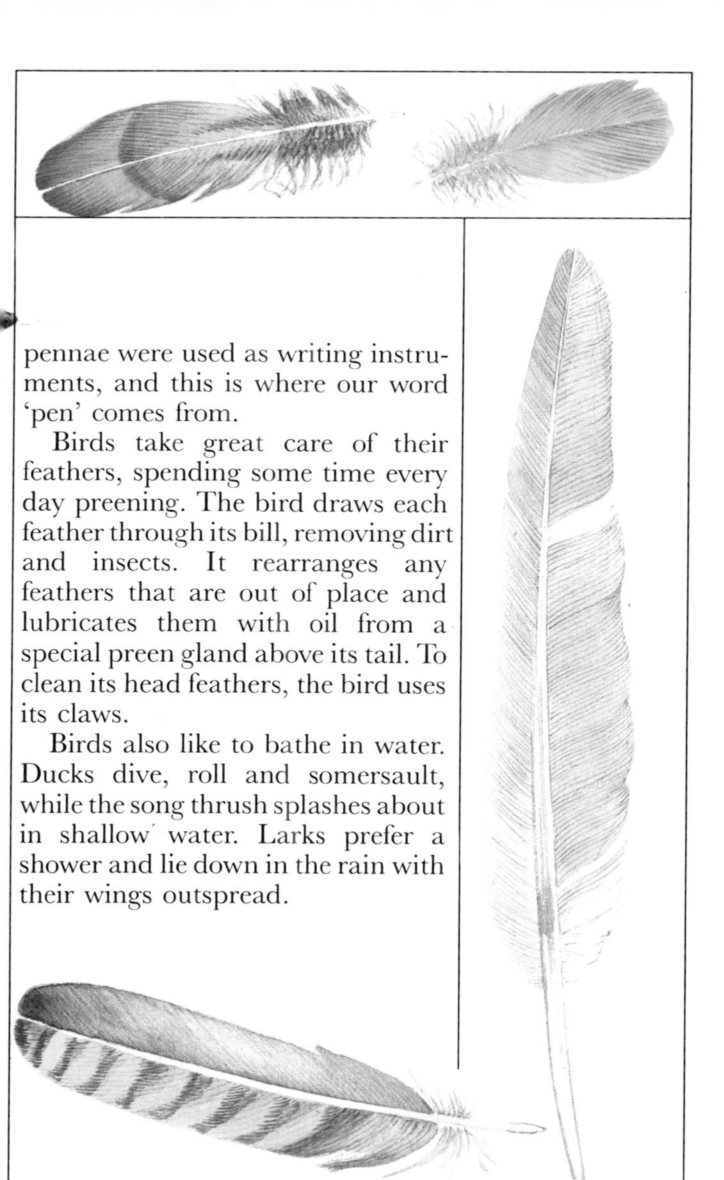

pennae were used as writing instruments, and this is where our word 'pen' comes from.

Birds take great care of their feathers, spending some time every day preening. The bird draws each feather through its bill, removing dirt and insects. It rearranges any feathers that are out of place and lubricates them with oil from a special preen gland above its tail. To clean its head feathers, the bird uses its claws.

Birds also like to bathe in water. Ducks dive, roll and somersault, while the song thrush splashes about in shallow water. Larks prefer a shower and lie down in the rain with their wings outspread.

Birds in flight

You can often identify a bird by the way it flies.

The swallow flies in graceful zig-zags, pursuing insects in the air. It keeps its forked tail closed when flying fast, and open when flying more slowly.

The crow flies in a straight line, flapping its great black wings.

The eagle soars on currents of air, flying in an upward spiral.

The kestrel often hovers in the air, looking for prey in the fields below.

The lark soars upwards in a wavering line, singing as it rises.

The wagtail descends to earth in rapid zig-zags.

The starling flies from one point to another in a straight line.

The tiny wren flies straight, its wings whirring.

The swallows twisting here and there
Round unseen corners of the air.

Andrew Young

The Skylark

The earth was green, the sky was blue:
I saw and heard one sunny morn
A skylark hang between the two,
A singing speck above the corn;

A stage below, in gay accord,
White butterflies danced on the wing,
And still the singing skylark soared,
And silent sank, and soared to sing.

Christina Rossetti

Vegetables

The country vegetables scorn
To lie about in shops,
They stand upright as they were born
In neatly patterned crops;

And when you want your dinner you
Don't buy it from a shelf,
You find a lettuce fresh with dew
And pull it for yourself;

You pick an apronful of peas
And shell them on the spot.
You cut a cabbage, if you please,
To pop into the pot.

The folk who their potatoes buy
From sacks before they sup,
Miss half of the potato's joy,
And that's to dig it up.

Eleanor Farjeon

In the garden

Summer, particularly early summer, is a busy time for the gardener: everything is growing so fast, including the weeds.

The gardener first aerates the soil, using a garden fork, and then the weeds must be hoed before they have a chance to grow. When the weather is dry, the garden has to be watered, preferably in the cool of the evening.

While some vegetables, flowers and fruits are ready for picking, others are still to be sown for an autumn crop. The soil is raked smooth and seeds sown in neat rows; or the gardener plants out the seedlings that have sprouted in the greenhouse.

A calendar of vegetables

	July	August	September
sow	weed		pick
courgettes			
broad beans			
leeks			
French beans			
cucumbers			
peas			
aubergines			

Generally, vegetables grow earlier in the south than in the north; so this calendar may vary by a few weeks according to where you live.

July **August** **September**

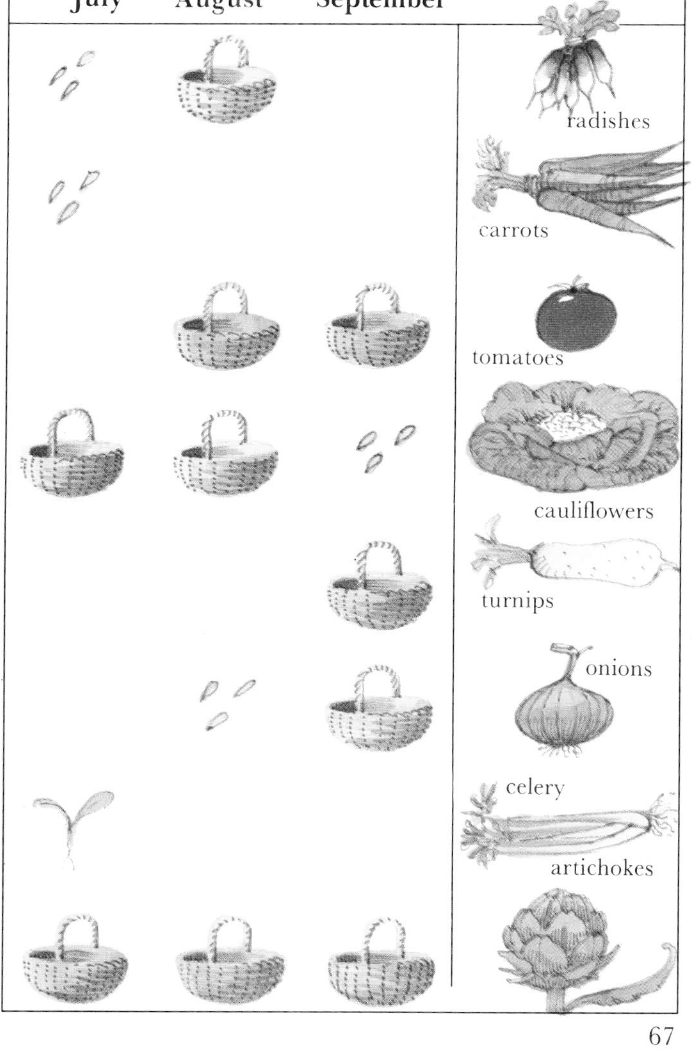

radishes

carrots

tomatoes

cauliflowers

turnips

onions

celery

artichokes

Herbs

Garden, show your shades of green . . .
Eleanor Farjeon

For hundreds of years, a herb garden would always be grown in any large garden. Herbs were grown for their scent, their flavour and for their medicinal qualities. Herbs grow readily in a sheltered spot and like well-drained soil and plenty of light.

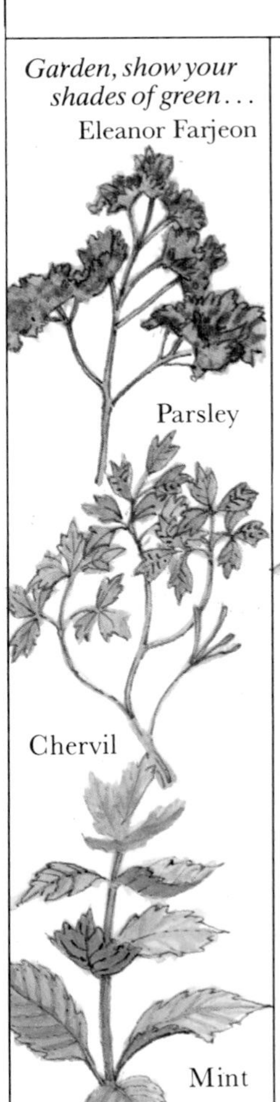

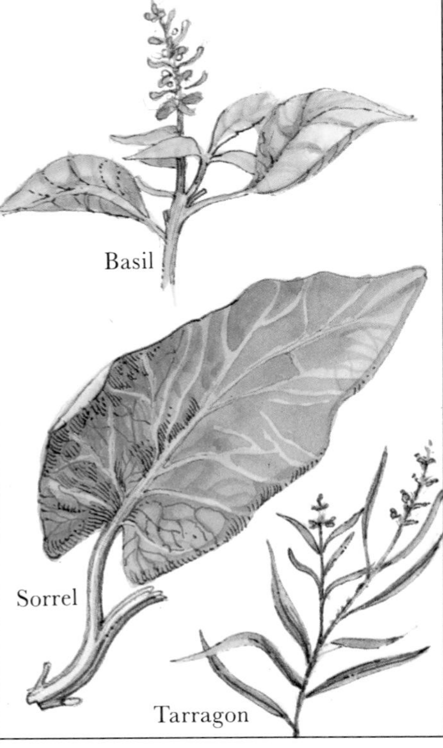

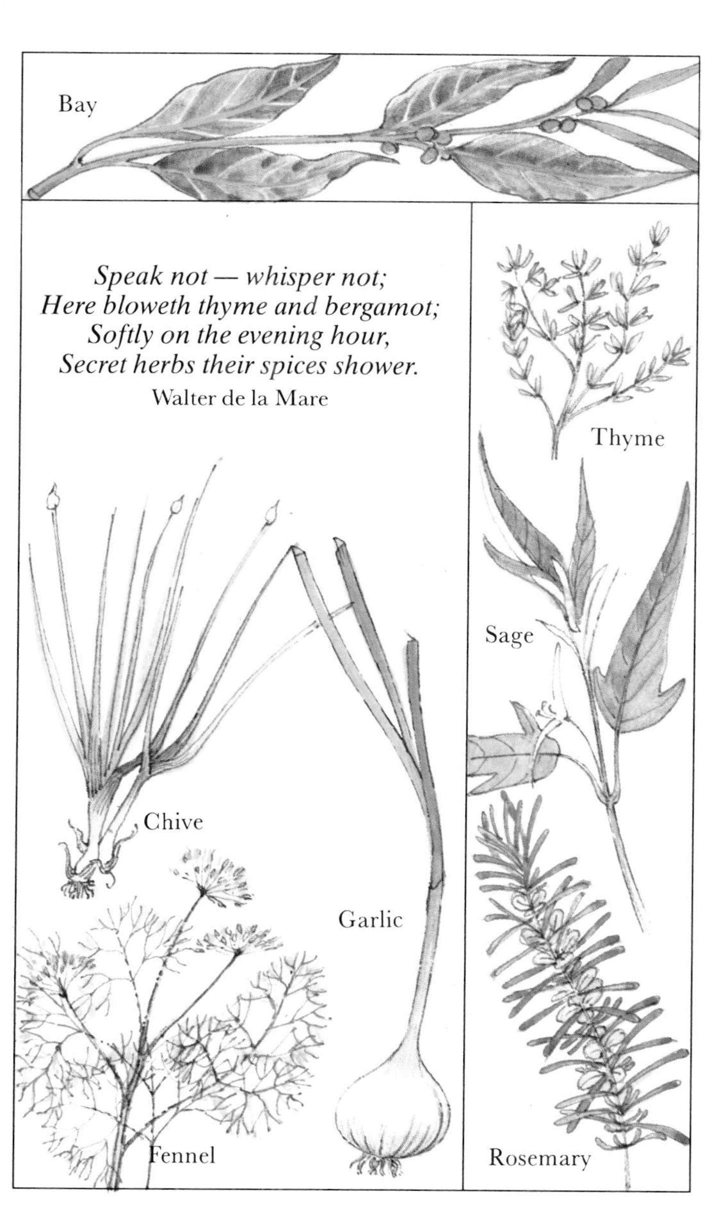
Bay
Speak not — whisper not;
Here bloweth thyme and bergamot;
Softly on the evening hour,
Secret herbs their spices shower.
Walter de la Mare
Thyme
Sage
Chive
Garlic
Fennel
Rosemary

Summer fruits

Summer brings us stone fruits: cherries appear first, followed by peaches, nectarines, apricots and plums.

The first soft fruits start to ripen in late spring and become plentiful in July and August: strawberries, raspberries, redcurrants and blackcurrants, gooseberries.

And in the shops we also find fruits grown in the Mediterranean countries, which have hotter summers than ours: melons, oranges, lemons, limes, grapes and olives.

Summer cooking

To make jam, choose fruit that is only just ripe: if it is too ripe, the jam may not set properly.

Apricot jam

For 2 medium-sized pots

1kg apricots
0.5kg sugar

Wash the apricots. Remove their stones. Put apricots and sugar into a thick-bottomed saucepan. Cook over low heat for about an hour, stirring from time to time.

To test whether the jam is ready, drop a little onto a cold plate. When it is cool, push it gently with your finger: if it crinkles and stays in the same place, the jam is ready. Ladle it into jars very carefully, jam is extremely hot. Cover them when cold.

Plum jam

1.5kg plums
1.5kg sugar
0.2l. water

Wash the plums, cut them in half and remove their stones. Cook them in the water until soft.

Add sugar and stir until it melts. Boil mixture fiercely for about 15 minutes. Test it as for apricot jam. Ladle it carefully into jars. Cool, then cover them.

The rule is, jam to-morrow and jam yesterday — but never jam today.

Lewis Carroll

Summer drink

Mash a banana well with a fork. Stir in the juice of an orange. Add a little water and one or two ice cubes. Decorate with mint.

Strawberry water-ice

½kg strawberries
½kg icing sugar
1 lemon

Wash the strawberries quickly. Sieve or liquidize them, then mix them well with the icing sugar and lemon juice. Pour into a metal tray or mould. Leave in freezer for at least two hours.

The hardest thing to do in the world

is stand in the hot sun
at the end of a long queue for
ice creams
watching all the people who've
just bought theirs
coming away from the queue
giving their ice creams their
very first lick.

Michael Rosen

Cheese

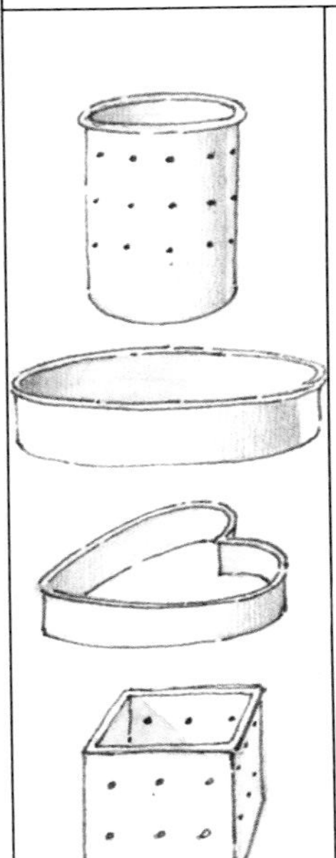

Milk turns sour quickly in hot weather. A long time ago, people discovered that they could still use sour milk if they made it into cheese. Sour milk curdles, separating into *curds* and *whey*. Nowadays a substance called *rennet* is usually added to milk to make it curdle. Rennet comes from the stomach of the cow.

The liquid whey is drained off, and the soft curds are made into cheese. Curds are drained, pressed and treated in different ways to make cheeses of different flavours and textures. They may be washed in salt water, wine, beer or a liqueur, flavoured with herbs or spices, or treated with a mould to make a blue cheese, such as Stilton.

Some cheeses, such as cottage cheese, are eaten fresh. But others are left in cellars to ripen. This can take a few weeks for a Cheshire, or two years for a mature Cheddar. Each kind of cheese needs a particular temperature and degree of moistness.

Some cheeses, such as Emmental, produce a gas as they ripen, causing holes to appear in the cheese.

Most of the cheese we eat is made of cows' milk; but the milk of other animals can be used too: goats, ewes, yaks, lamas, camels, water buffalo, mares.

The countries that make the most cheese are the U.S.A., U.S.S.R. and France. France alone produces about 300 kinds of cheese in all shapes and sizes, cubes, rounds, hearts, cones . . .

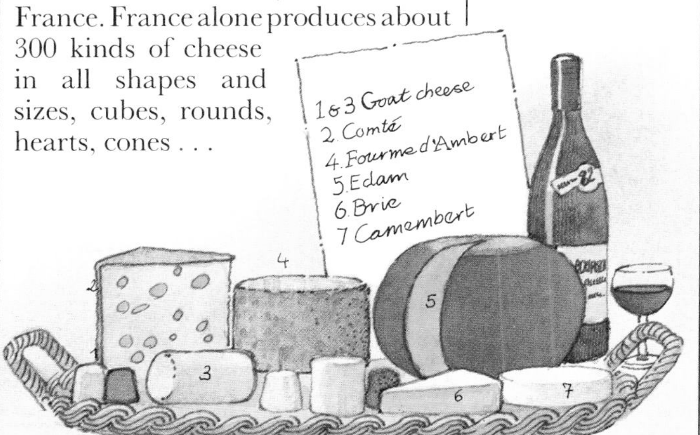

Wild flowers

Wild flowers grow almost anywhere in summer: meadows, fields, hedgerows, footpaths, riverbanks . . . and even out of cracks in the city pavement.

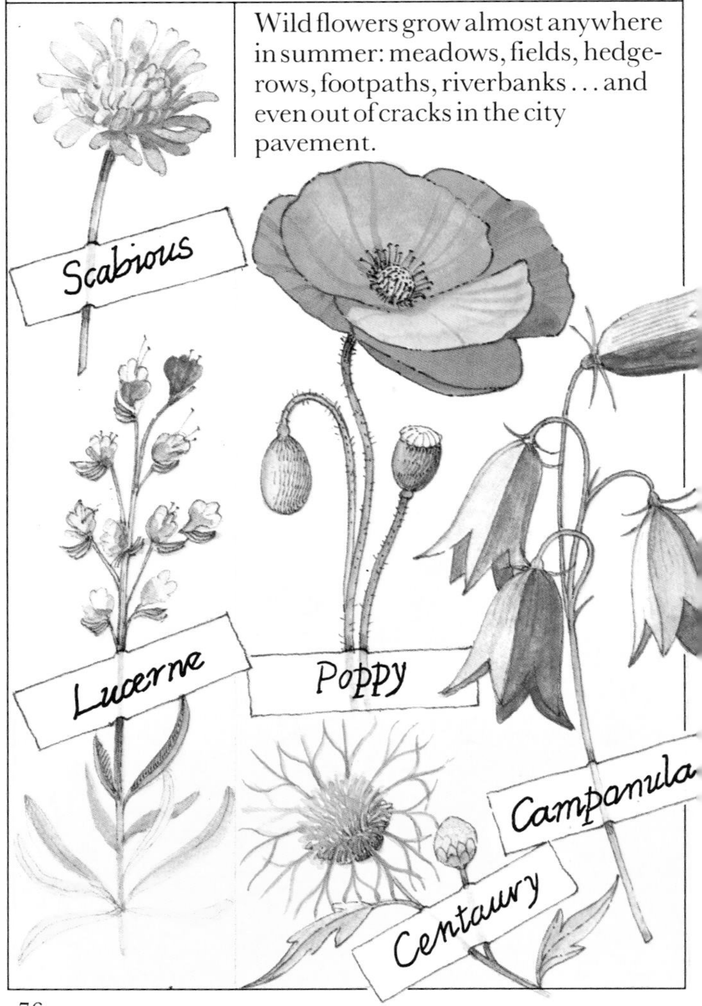

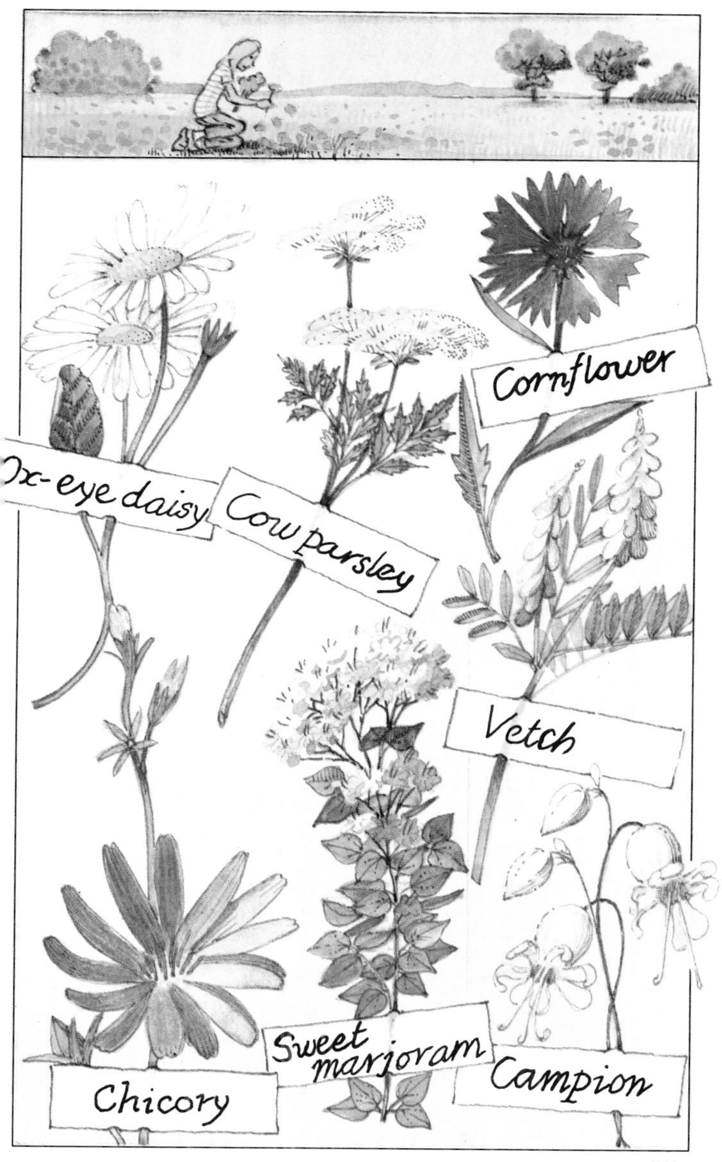
Cornflower
Ox-eye daisy
Cow parsley
Vetch
Sweet marjoram
Campion
Chicory

Grasses

Many kinds of grass and plant grow in fields and meadows, where they may be eaten by grazing farm animals or cut and dried by the farmer to be used as animal fodder in the winter.

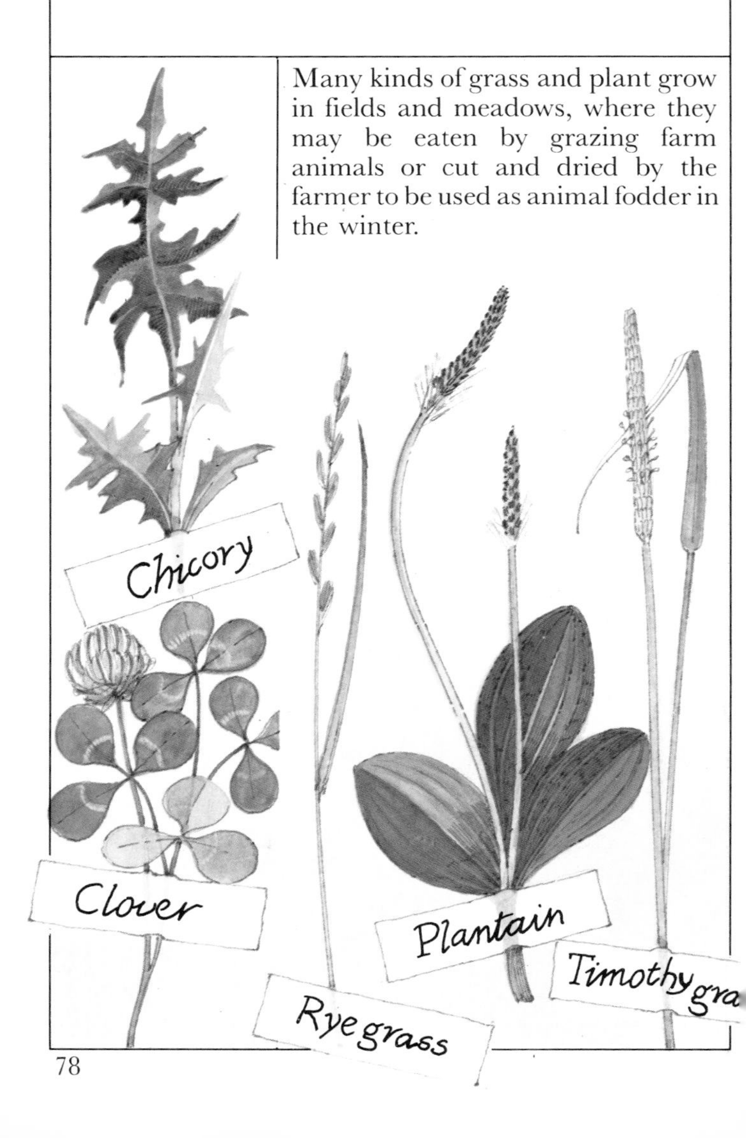

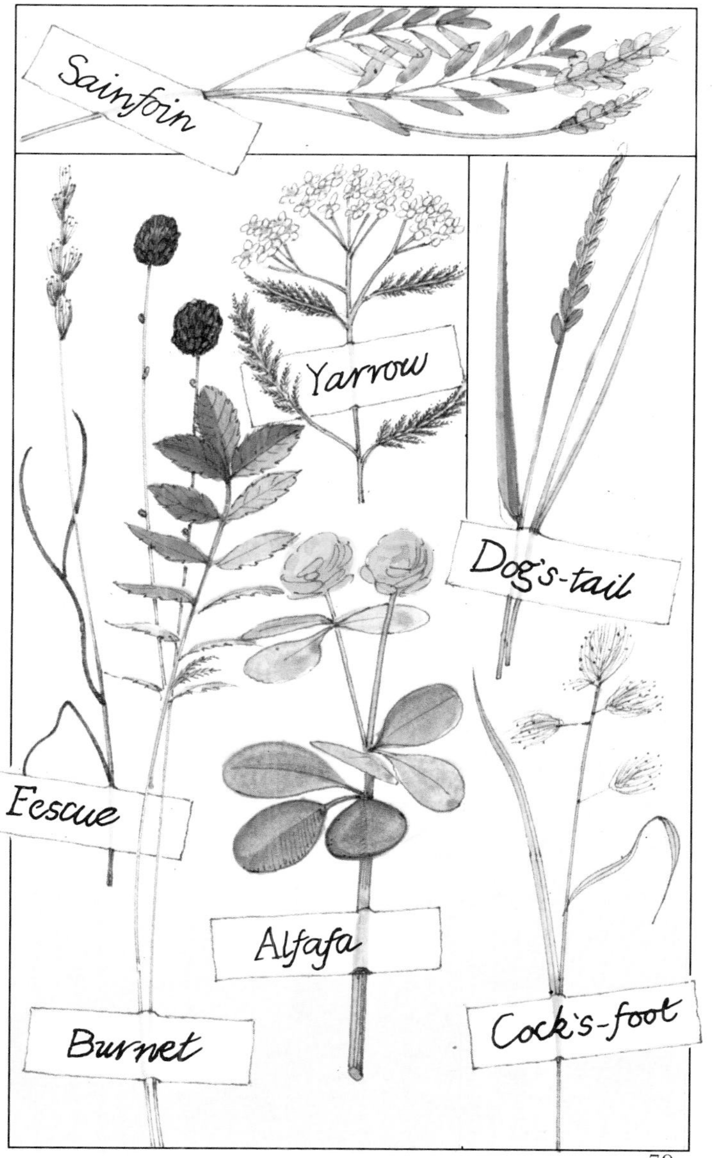
Sainfoin
Yarrow
Dog's-tail
Fescue
Alfafa
Burnet
Cock's-foot

Cereals

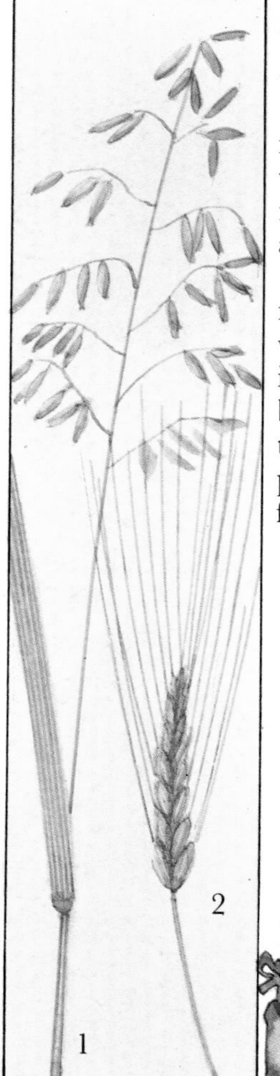

Farmers harvest their cereal crops before the autumn storms can wet the grain, causing it to rot.

Oats (1) are grown mainly to feed farm animals, and are a favourite with horses. We eat them in porridge, muesli and biscuits such as oat cakes and flapjacks.

Barley (2) can be grown in a wide range of climates. Much of the world's crop is fed to animals. Some is made into malt and used to make beer. The grain is sometimes added to soups and stews, and a kind of porridge can be made from barley flour.

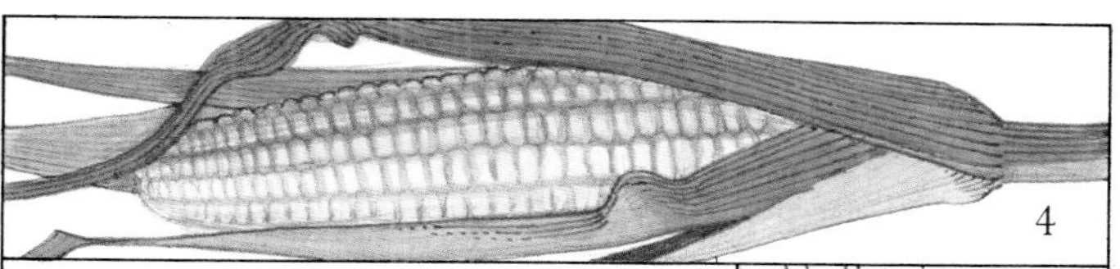

Rye (3) has long grains and, like barley, is bearded. Rye flour makes very dark bread, such as pumpernickel, which keeps longer than other bread. It is sometimes mixed with wheat flour in baking. Rye is used to make crispbreads and is also fed to animals. It is the hardiest of the cereals and will grow in cold places on poor soil.

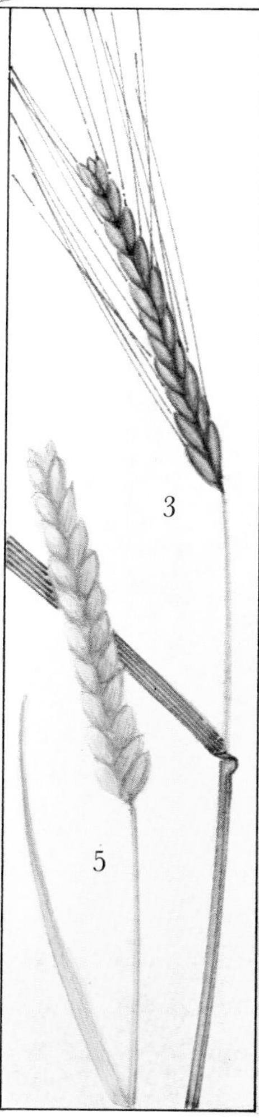

Corn or maize (4) comes originally from America. Animals eat it. So do we, as sweetcorn, popcorn and in cornflakes. Cornflour, which is very fine, is used in sauces and puddings.

Wheat (5) is the world's chief cereal crop. Most of the bread we eat is made from wheat; so are many breakfast cereals. Hard types of wheat grow in hot, dry places. These are used to make semolina, spaghetti and other kinds of pasta. The everyday flour we use in baking and cooking comes from the softer types of wheat that need less heat to grow.

The harvest

Summer brings the harvest. After all their work in the fields, the farmers can gather in their crops.

In the old days grain was cut with scythes, gathered into sheaves or bundles with sickles, then tied and left in the fields to dry. It was then taken back to the farm for threshing, when the sheaves were beaten to separate the grain from the chaff and straw.

The end of harvest was a time of celebration. Country people feasted and made merry. The last sheaf was often hung on the barn or farmhouse door for good luck until the following year.

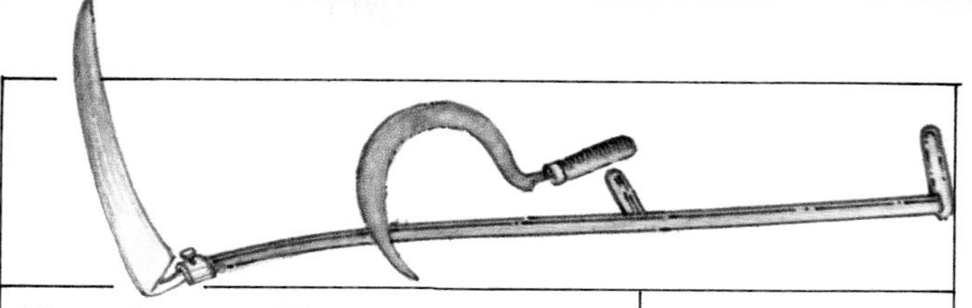

A scythe and a sickle

Nowadays combine-harvesters do all the work. They cut and they thresh, collecting the grain into a big grain tank and leaving the straw behind. A pick-up baler then gathers the straw and packs it into bundles.

The boughs do shake and the
bells do ring,
So merrily comes our harvest in,

We've ploughed, we've sowed,
We've reaped, we've mowed,
We've got our harvest in.

Anon.

A summer dictionary

August
August was named after an emperor: Augustus Caesar, the first of the Roman emperors, who lived 2000 years ago.

Basil
In the old days people kept dried basil around the house to keep away insects.

Beetles
Beetles have mouths that bite. Different varieties eat plants, insects, carrion, dung, bark, wool, wood, fur, feathers, even carpets.

Bugs
Bugs have mouths like hollow needles that suck. Their food is generally liquid: the sap of plants or blood of animals.

Ceres
Ceres was the Roman goddess of agriculture. From her name comes the word cereal, which means edible grain.

Cicada
The male cicada is the loudest insect in the world. In North America there is a cicada that spends 17 years as a larva underground. It lives for only a few weeks as an adult.

Corn-dollies
People once believed it unlucky to cut the last of the corn in a field. They plaited the uncut stalks into a corn-dolly and took turns throwing the sickle at it, so that everyone took part in cutting the last of the corn. Another custom was to keep the dolly till the following year and bury it in the field for luck on Plough Monday, the day on which farm workers went back to the plough after the Christmas holidays.

Daddy-long-legs
Crane-flies are known as daddy-

long-legs. With their six long legs they hang from plants and grasses. And they seem able to manage if they lose one, two or even three legs.

Dog-star

The dog-star, Sirius, is the brightest in the southern sky. There is a period in July and August when it rises and sets at about the same time as the sun. The ancient Romans called these days the dog-days, thinking that it was hot because the heat of the dog-star was added to that of the sun. In fact stars are too far away to give the Earth much heat.

Eagle

In summer the nestlings of the golden eagle fly away from their nest, leaving it full of bones. These are the remains of the meals their parents have brought them for the past three months. Eagles eat hares, birds, carrion and even lambs. Their nest, built somewhere high, such as a mountain crag, looks like a huge basket made of sticks. They add to it each year. In North America a bald eagle's nest once came down during a storm. It was 35 years old and was thought to weigh about 1818 kg.

Ears

Mosquitoes have ears on their antennae. Crickets and cicadas have ears on their front legs and grasshoppers on the sides of their abdomens.

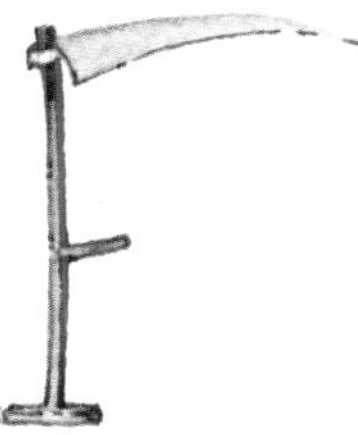

Flowers

If cut flowers begin to look limp, try trimming the stalks and soaking the ends in boiling water. Then return the flowers to fresh water. They may revive.

Fox

A fox's underground home is called an earth. In summer the cubs come out of the earth to play. They pounce on small animals, like beetles. By the time the cold weather comes, they will be hunting larger animals and fending for themselves.

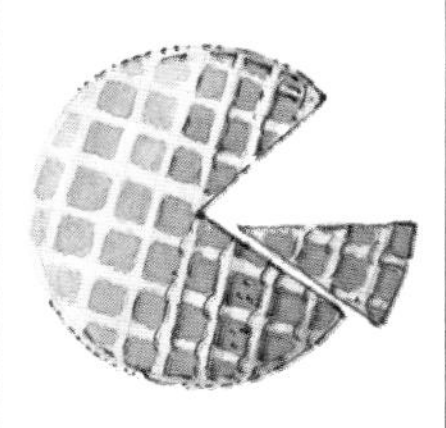

Grasshopper

The female grasshopper lays her eggs in the soil in late summer. They hatch the following spring.

The Grasshopper,
The Grasshopper,
I will explain to you:-

He is the Brownies' racehorse,
The Fairies' Kangaroo.
Vachel Lindsay

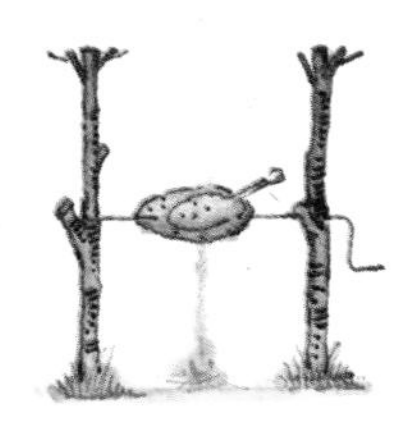

Harvest moon

The full moon around the time of the autumn equinox is called a harvest moon. It rises at about sunset for several days, lighting harvesters who work into the night.

Harvest mouse

The harvest mouse supports itself, as it climbs up and down stalks of corn, by twisting its tail round the stalks. It can even hang by its tail.

Ice-house

Before refrigerators were invented, people collected ice in winter and stored it in ice-houses. These were built underground and had thick walls and ceilings to keep them cool.

Insects

Nearly a million kinds of insect are known. An insect's body is divided into three parts: head, thorax and abdomen. It has six legs and a pair of antennae.

July

July was named after the Roman soldier and statesman, Julius Caesar.

June

June was probably named after Juno, the Roman goddess of women.

Knot

In late summer, as other birds leave to escape the winter, knots begin to arrive from the Arctic, where they breed. They spend the winter in Britain, on marshes and estuaries. In summer they are mottled black and chestnut above, russet below. In winter they become grey above, whitish below.

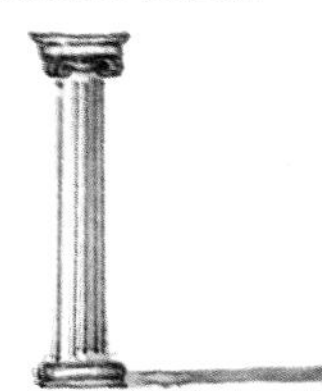

Lammas day

At the beginning of the harvest, the Saxons had a feast of thanksgiving. It was called 'hlaefmaesse', which means loaf-mass. This became Lammas day, celebrated by the

Christian Church every year on 1 August. Services of thanksgiving are now held after harvest.

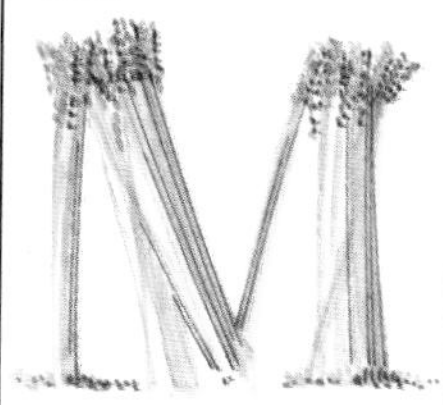

Mining bee

The mining bee digs her nest underground, where she lays her eggs on little balls of pollen and nectar. The larvae feed on the nest when they hatch. The mining bee is solitary: she makes her nest and feeds her young herself, unlike the honey bee who lives and works in colonies.

Night

Night is come,
Owls are out;
Beetles hum
Round about.
Children snore
Safe in bed,
Nothing more
Need be said.
Sir Henry Newbolt

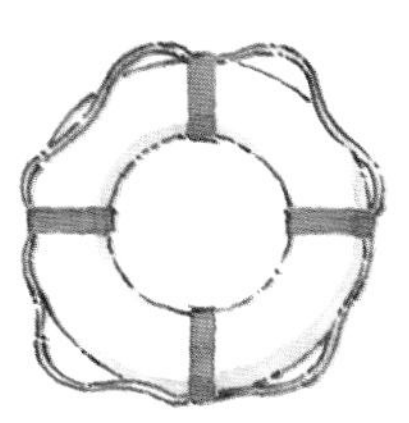

Oystercatchers

Oystercatchers live on the shore and feed on shellfish which they prise open with their long orange bills. Strangely enough, they do not eat oysters. In spring and summer groups of these black and white birds form circles and run up and down, pointing their bills to the ground and calling, 'kleep-kleep'.

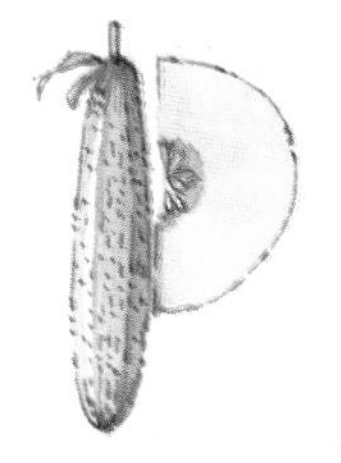

Painted lady butterfly

This butterfly flies over the Channel from the Continent to spend the summer in Britain, where it may be seen between May and October.

Queen Anne's lace

This wild flower is also called cow parsley or wild carrot. It is the ancestor of the carrot we eat.

Queen Anne, Queen
  Anne,
has washed her lace
(She chose a
  summer's day)
And hung it in grassy
  place
To whiten, if it may.
Mary Leslie Newton

River

Summer river:
Though there's a bridge,
my horse
Prefers the ford.
Shiki

Rhubarb

A rhubarb leaf
makes a very good hat,
or a parasol,
so remember that
if the sun shines down
on your sunburned nose . . .
and you happen to know
where rhubarb grows.
Aileen Fisher

Sting

When a bee stings you, it dies. This is because its sting is barbed and sticks in the flesh, tearing off part of the bee's abdomen as it flies away. Wasps can sting many times.

Swallows

Swallows come to Britain for the spring and summer, when there are plenty of insects to eat. They fly to South Africa for the winter.

Fly away, fly away, over the sea,
Sun-loving swallow, for summer is done.
Come again, come again,
come back to me,
Bringing the summer
and bringing the sun.
Christina Rossetti

Swift

The swift spends more time in the air than any other land bird: it does not come to earth for nine months or more, but feeds on flying insects. Its legs are used so little that they are very weak. Swifts winter in Africa.

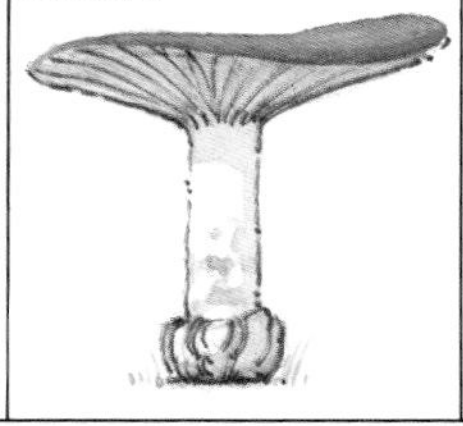

Thatch

In the middle ages most people's roofs were thatched. Thatch is made of straw or reeds, which were cheap and provided good insulation. Straw is also fed to animals and used for their bedding. Once people stuffed mattresses with straw.

Ultraviolet

The sun gives out invisible rays of ultraviolet light. These rays can be created scientifically to treat various illnesses, but if your skin is exposed to ultraviolet light for too long it will burn.

Velvet ants

Velvet ants are really wasps. But the females have no wings and look like ants. They lay their eggs in a bumble bee's nest underground and feed on the bee's honey stores. When the velvet ant larvae hatch, they eat the bumble bee larvae.

Water spider

The water spider spins an underwater web among weeds. It lives and breathes in an underwater air bubble that the spider has created little by little from air that it carries trapped between its hind legs and hairy body. It darts out from its web to catch water insects and brings them back to eat in the air bubble.

Wings

Bees have four
wings,
birds have two,
I haven't any
and that's too few.
Aileen Fisher

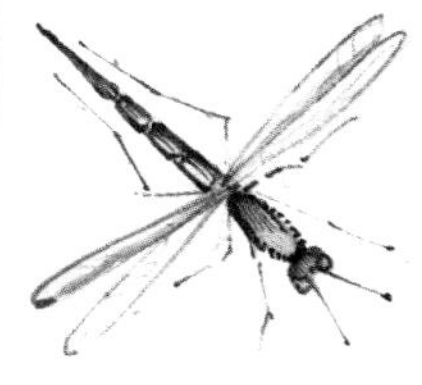

Xylophage

A xylophage is a wood-eating insect. It leaves little holes in wood.

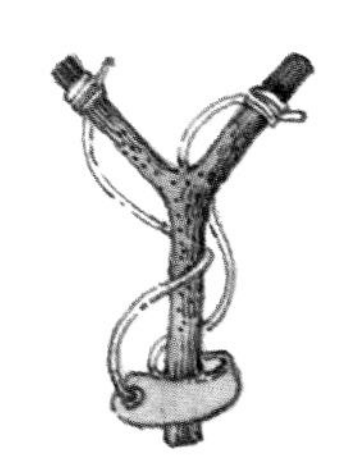

Year

Our year lasts 365¼ days, the time it takes the Earth to travel round the sun. Other planets have longer of shorter years. Mercury's journey round the sun takes 88 days, Pluto's 247 years.

Zenith

At noon in summer the sun is at its zenith, the highest point above us in the sky. Its rays shine directly down on us and this is the hottest time of day.

Biography

Jean Claverie, the illustrator of *Summer,* lives in a village near Lyons in France with his wife, who is also a well-known illustrator, and their two young sons. He divides his time between illustrating books, for French, German and British publisers, and teaching at the Lyons College of Art. He is one of France's leading and best-loved artists working in children's books.

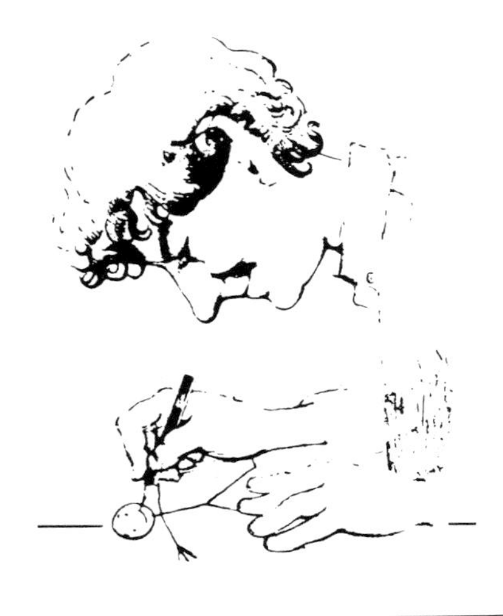

Acknowledgements

The editor and publishers wish to thank the following for permission to use copyright material:

The author for *Back to School* by Allan Ahlberg from Please Mrs Butler, Kestrel Books 1983; E. Morris for *High Summer on the Mountains* by Idris Davies; Jonathan Cape Ltd. for *The Green Tent, School's Out* by W.H. Davies from Complete Poems 1963; Cresset Press Ltd. and Miss E.J. Scovell for *The Boy Fishing* by E.J. Scovell from Shadows of Chrysanthemums; Curtis Brown Ltd. for *I think that life would be more fun...* by Ogden Nash; Doubleday & Co. Inc. for *Sing a song of picnics* by Rachel Field from Taxis and Toadstools © 1926 by the Century Company; Gerald Duckworth & Co. ltd. for *The Vulture* by Hilaire Belloc from More Beasts for Worse Children; The Estate of Eleanor Farjeon for *Nine O'Clock Bells, The night will never stay* from Silver-Sand and Snow, Michael Joseph Ltd., and for *Vegetables* from poems for Children, Lippincott; Faber & Faber Ltd. for *The grass is happy*... by Ted Hughes from Season Songs 1976; Harcourt Brace & World Inc. for *Lesson from a Sundial* rendered from the German by Louis Untermayer from Rainbow in the Sky, edited by Louis Untermayer © renewed 1963; Harper & Row Públishers for *How Big, Lady of Night, Speaking of Leaves*, and *Wings* by Aileen Fisher from Out in the Dark and Daylight, and for *Here Comes*... by Shel Silverstein from A Light in the Attic and *No they never see*... from Snowmen; the author for *O the sky's an umbrella*... from The Waves by William Jay Smith; Houghton Mifflin Co. for *The Fishing Pole* by Mary Carolyn Davies from A Little Freckled Person, and for *The Lizard* by Abbie Farwell Brown from Songs of Sixpence; The Literary Trustees of Walter de la Mare for *Speak not-whisper not*... from Complete Poems, Faber © 1969; McGraw Hill Book Co. for *In this quiet pool* by William Moore from Little Raccoon and Poems from the Woods; Arthur S. Pederson, trustees Estate Rachel Field Pederson for *I saw the sea*... From A Summer Morning by Rachel Field, Macmillan & Co. New York; Ivor S. Roberts for *Firefly, The People* by Elizabeth Madox Roberts from Under the Tree, Viking © 1950; the author for *The Hardest Thing to do in the World* by Michael Rosen from You Tell Me, Kestrel Books, 1979; Random House Publishing Co. for *Summer Serenade* by Ogden Nash © Ogden Nash; Secker & Warburg Ltd. for *The Swallows* by Andrew Young from Complete Poems 1974; Sidgwick & Jackson Ltd. for *Sun-shade* by A.E. Housman from Collected Poems 1937; Hodder & Stoughton Ltd for *Night is Come* by Sir Henry Newbolt from Finis.

Every effort has been made to trace copyright but if any omissions have been made please let us know in order that we may put it right in the next edition.